Grateful

ALSO BY DIANA BUTLER BASS

Grounded
Christianity After Religion
A People's History of Christianity
Christianity for the Rest of Us

DIANA
BUTLER BASS

Grateful

THE SUBVERSIVE PRACTICE
OF GIVING THANKS

HarperOne
An Imprint of HarperCollinsPublishers

HarperOne

FIRST HARPERCOLLINS PAPERBACK EDITION PUBLISHED IN 2019

Designed by Michelle Crowe

Library of Congress Cataloging-in-Publication Data is available upon request.

ISBN 978-0-06-265948-4

21 22 23   LSC   10 9 8 7 6 5 4

To Roger Freet

Thank you for your encouragement, your friendship,
and your unfailing belief in the power of words.

For all that has been—thanks.
For all that shall be—yes.

—DAG HAMMARSKJÖLD

Let gratitude be the pillow upon which you
kneel to say your nightly prayer.
And let faith be the bridge you build to overcome evil and welcome good.

—MAYA ANGELOU

CONTENTS

Confession: No Thanks

Gratitude is the memory of the heart.

—FRENCH PROVERB

I pulled the card from the envelope, appreciatively fingering its velvety thickness. It was formal and traditional, the sort one rarely sees anymore, with a single word embossed on the front: "Grateful."

I opened it and read, "Thank you for the lovely thank-you note!"

I read it again, just to make sure. It was a thank-you note for a thank-you note.

Now what?

Do you send a thank-you note for the thank-you note received for sending a thank-you note? Was there a rule for this? I have never been very good at these things. Writing the original note was hard enough; I considered it a mannerly triumph. But what happens when someone thanks you for saying thanks? Should you return thanks *again*? "This could go on forever," I sighed. I held the kind note in my hand, not knowing what was right or proper. Saying thank you can be so complicated.

Suddenly, I felt a bit like that little girl whose mother forced her to write thank-you notes for Christmas and birthday gifts. I was not good at it. I did not want to do it, and I did not know what to say. But when she sat me down and insisted, I wrote, usually scrawling "Thanks" and "Love, Diana" in tipsy letters on the note cards supplied for the exercise. I must have complained quite a bit, because one Christmas an etiquette book showed up as a gift under the tree. A bookmark was not so subtly placed before the section "How to Write Thank-You Notes." I got the point, but I did not improve in practice.

Years later, the struggle over thank-you notes repeated with my own daughter. Although I had not been good at it, I hoped she would be. No such luck. She resisted and complained just as I had at her age. I bought her fancy cards and personalized stationery, supplied her with colored pens and cute stickers, hoping all might inspire notes of gratitude. It did not work. She utterly refused to write. However, no *Miss Manners* showed up under the Christmas tree. Instead, I prompted her to call gift givers and send thank-you e-mails. We had some success with electronic forms of expressing gratitude, but only minimally so. I gave up. When I stopped resorting to threats and etiquette shaming, she stopped writing thank-you notes. Is there DNA for ingratitude? For daughter wound up like mother, and I felt bad that I had not done better as a parent.

I have always struggled with gratitude. I want to be grateful, but too often I find myself with no thanks.

Oddly enough, whatever my shortcomings in practice, the concept of gratitude still captivated me. Although I rarely sent thank-you notes as a girl, I collected pretty stationery designed for that very purpose. I loved when people brought my mother thank-you gifts of flowers or food after she volunteered at church or hosted a dinner party. When I was a teenager, I tried to memorize every verse in the New Testament about thanks. It seemed the Christian sort of thing to do. Of the dozens of mentions of gratitude in its pages, I managed to memorize only one: "In everything give thanks" (1 Thess. 5:18, KJV). I proudly quoted it to a church friend. She replied, "But that's only half the verse!" That's not a very high success rate—one-half of one verse on thanksgiving.

I remember listening to a guest on *The Oprah Winfrey Show* discussing the power of gratitude to change one's life. A sort of spiritual longing arose in my heart. I felt inspired and decided to keep a gratitude journal. That lasted less than a week. On another occasion, I embarked upon the noble project of making a moment of gratitude part of our family's bedtime ritual. We did it once. And then there is that painful Thanksgiving dinner exercise in which no one eats until everyone at the table says something they are thankful for. It is supposed to remind us about the real meaning of the holiday. But it feels more like a turkey hostage situation than a spiritual exercise in grace. I feel thankful when it ends.

You can only attempt something for so long before you give up. By the time I received the thank-you note for my thank-you note, I had consigned myself to life as a gratitude klutz.

I confess. I gave up on thanks. I tossed the "Grateful" card on a pile of correspondence. I never replied.

FLUNKING GRATITUDE

In late 2015, I was working on a project about spirituality and character. A pile of books sat on my desk—about virtues like charity, joy, kindness, patience, and thankfulness. Next to them was a survey examining American religion and spirituality. I thumbed through its pages, and a question caught my attention:

> How often do you feel a strong sense of gratitude or
> thankfulness? Would you say at least once a week,
> once or twice a month, several times a year, seldom,
> or never?[1]

"Interesting," I thought. Then I read the answer: an astonishing 78 percent of Americans responded by saying that they had felt *strongly* thankful in the last week!

A wave of guilt engulfed me. I was not sure I was one of them. I shoved the survey aside.

My glance fell on the other books. Half of them had the word "gratitude," "thanks," or "thankfulness" in the title. The volumes seemed to stare back at me, their cheerful bright covers adorned with pictures of flowers and smiling faces. Several promised happiness, healing, success, or personal fulfillment. The collection was a self-help heap of thanks, a perky pile of gratefulness. The stack seemed to scold me, wagging accusing authorial fingers in my direction, as if knowing I had flunked the gratitude exam. I half expected my late mother's ghost, straight from Christmas past, to appear and regift me with that etiquette guide.

What kind of horrible person was I? Somehow, "gratitude klutz" no longer seemed adequate. Was I an ingrate? An ugly word. No one wants to be an ingrate. But I realized that I rarely experienced or thought about gratitude. Did I truly not have moments of gratefulness? Or did they bypass me without recognition? I did not know.

Whatever the case, that 78 percent made me feel lonely.

And curious. I mentioned the survey to several friends. Their responses were remarkably similar to mine: "What?" "Eight out of ten?" "People don't seem *that* grateful."

One of those friends is a sociologist. "I don't believe it," I insisted to him. "Nearly 80 percent of Americans say they feel deep gratitude at least once a week?" Could that possibly be true?

Gratitude researchers claim that if we are grateful, we are happier and more content, that there is a social consequence to thankfulness. "I don't see that," I said to my friend. "Other data say we are angry, discontented, and unsatisfied. And our politics isn't exactly based in gratitude. 'Thank you' doesn't seem to be our strength right now."

He chuckled and then explained: "Whenever eight in ten Americans answer the same way on a question, the question becomes less valuable for analysis. It also makes you suspect that there is serious social desirability bias going on here."

A "social desirably bias" occurs when people answer a question in a way that makes them look good to themselves or others, that matches the image of the person they aspire to be. In other words, that high percentage might indicate there are many people, like me, who know that gratitude is good and want to be grateful, to feel gratitude, or to be seen as thankful people. We believe gratitude is virtuous. We might experience gratitude in a given moment and say to a pollster, "Yes, I felt thankful." But inwardly, we know how difficult it is to practice and sustain thanksgiving—to live a truly grateful *life*.

No matter how we answer the question during a particular week, many of us remember our parents' nagging, that stash of thank-you notes in the back of a desk drawer, shortening the Thanksgiving dinner prayer, or forgetting to let our grandparents know how much we appreciated their gifts. There is a gap between what we believe and what we practice. Many of us feel guilty when it comes to gratitude.

My questions mounted: What is gratitude? And why is it so hard? Does being thankful really change things? Could our lives be different if we were more grateful? Might a new understanding of gratitude open a way of healing and compassion—both for ourselves and for those around us?

I did not know the answers. But a sense of urgency gripped me, and I wanted to find out.

"ME" AND "WE"

For as much as I struggle with practicing gratitude in my life, a far larger problem affects us all. I kept thinking about the 78 percent of Americans who said they felt "a strong sense of gratitude" at least once a week—that number represents nearly 90 percent of Christians, almost 70 percent of adherents of other world religions, and 60 percent of atheists who answered the survey. Whatever theology or doctrine divides us, a large majority share a common belief that giving thanks is good.

That sounds great, but those numbers also point to a problem: that of a gratitude gap. They reveal a disparity between our private feelings and our public attitudes. Social scientists have extolled gratitude as a personal path to peace, health, and contentment. Giving thanks, however, is more than a private practice; those same researchers insist that gratitude is socially beneficial and strengthens communities. Gratitude is about "me," and it is about "we." Where is the gap? A week after the Pew survey on the gratitude question, Public Religion Research Institute posted a very different study regarding American attitudes as we moved into a presidential election year. That study discovered that Americans were more anxious, less optimistic, and more distrustful than ever. Subsequent political events made evident a surge of rage, revealing a toxic level of anger, fear, division, and intolerance in the American electorate.[2]

The surveys puzzled me. Did the same people who felt grateful also express these negative emotions? Had they divided their lives into personal thanks and public rage? But can gratitude ever really be private? Shouldn't it have meaningful impact on families, communities, and the society in which we live?

Thus, I began to see two issues surrounding gratitude. The first involves "me." Why is it hard to practice gratitude in meaningful and sustained ways? Many may feel grateful, but they are equally aware of the difficulty in expressing thanks to family, friends, and kind strangers. We recognize and appreciate gifts directed toward us, but we often struggle with how to respond. On a personal level, as I readily admit from my own experience, gratitude can be challenging.

The second concern involves "we." What might it mean to live together as a thankful society? As human beings, we possess an intuitive awareness that we depend on others to survive. We are safer and happier when we care for each other in community, when we do things for each other. If we recognize mutuality, we experience gratitude as central to civic life. When we work together, when we share, and when we care, there is enough for all. We appreciate each other for what we all contribute to flourishing communities. And we appreciate one another for the good gifts of life. Whether you write a thank-you note to Grandma does not matter much in this larger sense, but how you—how *we*—appreciate the ties that bind us as a larger society matters greatly to everyone. How we live together in and with gratitude makes all the difference in the world. Indeed, living gratefully makes the world different.

I may struggle with personal gratitude. You may wrestle with giving thanks. A quick glance at the news, however, demonstrates that we are failing at communal thanksgiving. We are anxious and angry, because we are haunted by nightmares of scarcity, dystopian fears that someone else is taking everything, that there is never enough, and we will never get what we think we deserve. In wealthy societies that fear is, in many ways, stoked by real economic inequality and political injustice, resulting in cravings for things we think will fill us, fix us, or make us forget our doubts and pain. This leads to all sorts of addictive behaviors with drugs, sex, alcohol, money, shopping, food, hoarding, and violence. Our fears and disappointments mount, merging with those of our neighbors, and become the seedbed for politics of protection, limits, and rage. This is not a vision of a community of gratitude. We are a society of ingrates.[3]

In November 2015, both surveys measured something true. One survey measured private gratitude; the other measured the absence of communal gratefulness. *I* prize gratitude; *I* experience it; *I* appreciate when someone does *me* a favor or gives *me* a gift. *I feel strongly grateful when something good happens to me.* At the same time, however, as a society, *we* are being driven by the opposite impulse, the sense of powerlessness that comes from thinking we will never have what we deserve or want: "We are held captive by dissatisfaction."[4] This is the gratitude gap: we may be thankful in private, but individual gratefulness does not appear to make much difference in our larger common life. Giving thanks may be personally rewarding, but larger forces have extinguished beneficial forms of gratitude from our economic and political lives. We recognize gifts and are grateful on an ad hoc basis, but the world in which we live is surely not shaped by such thankfulness. No, we live in a toxic habitat of ingratitude. Nothing really escapes its poison.

Even the most grateful of us cannot survive long in such an environment. Can we clean up this mess?

CHEAP GRATITUDE

I am a historian. When I am perplexed, I often look to the past for understanding. Many commentators have pointed out parallels between our times and the 1930s in Germany. Often such comparisons are overblown, but one similarity intrigues me. Then, a citizenry well-versed in a theology of grace—the idea that all good things come from God—had turned gratitude into a path of individual salvation and personal comfort, all the while allowing deep social discontent and anger to fester in public life.

A young pastor named Dietrich Bonhoeffer noticed this gap. He accused his fellow Germans of embracing a diminished form of thankfulness. He called it "cheap grace." Pastor Bonhoeffer began to preach about the importance of a costly faith that embodied a transformative practice of gratitude. The result was one of the most influential and bestselling books ever written on the spiritual life, *The Cost of Discipleship*. Later, when he was in prison for resisting Hitler, Bonhoeffer experienced gratitude, a sense of humility and dependence on the gifts of others, more profoundly than ever before:

> In normal life one is not at all aware that we always receive infinitely more than we give, and that gratitude is what enriches life. One easily overestimates the importance of one's own acts and deeds, compared with what we become only through other people.[5]

"Normal" life in Western society, even eighty years ago, obscured what was true and important about the nature of things: that life is an abundance of shared gifts. We do not really achieve. We receive. We give to each other. We are grateful.

Analogies to anything that happened in 1930s Germany are, of course, notoriously alarmist. But it seems entirely possible that Bonhoeffer described something that just will not go away in Western societies. "Cheap gratitude" plagues us. Our understanding of thanks is polluted by our toxic dissatisfactions as we praise God for material possessions instead of the good gifts of nature and neighbor. Much of what passes for gratitude today appears to be a sort of secular prosperity gospel. If we just say "Thank you, thank you, thank you" long enough and with the greatest sincerity, we will be healthy and wealthy. This form of gratitude acts as a magical mantra, the key to unlocking personal spiritual peace and well-being. If we feel just good enough, with enough money and success, life will be a blessing. Or maybe not. Maybe we want just a bit more. A bit more blessing. What could be wrong with that?

In addition to prosperity gratitude, there is another kind of cheap gratitude: the sort based in duty or demand. If someone gives you a gift, you must return the favor. You owe a debt. Duty-based gratitude is emotionally empty and causes resentment. It is easy to suspect that benefits are given to exert control by, or forge loyalty to, an unscrupulous benefactor. Obligatory gratitude rarely has a heart. Rather, it breeds contempt and fosters injustice. In a real way, duty and debt cheapen gratitude to a social or political indenture.

These conceptions of gratitude—that of a privatized spirituality of success or a binding duty of obligation—have contributed to the gratitude deficit. One seems almost too easy, the other too hard. We feel grateful when someone does us a favor or when greeted by a beautiful sunrise, but personal gratitude does not seem to make a difference beyond a limited sphere. Public life is for those who get and take what they can.

DEEPLY GRATEFUL

When I assessed my struggles with gratitude honestly, I realized that I did not understand what it really was, other than a parental requirement to write thank-you notes. That lack of understanding has led to my many flawed attempts to integrate practices of thankfulness into my life, and my failed experiments at practicing appreciation skewed my perception of gratefulness.

Recently, I asked a group of people to define gratitude. They came up with more than fifty different definitions and ideas. Some thought it was a feeling, others thought it was a practice, and still others considered it a moral disposition; only a few identified gratitude as a civic obligation. Some said it was human and universal, while still others insisted it must be part of a specific religion. Do we comprehend what gratitude is? Seventy-eight percent of Americans said that they had felt it in the last week, but apparently we cannot agree on what "it" is. And that is hard to admit—that we might not share any common understanding of this thing most of us claim to value.

Can we know gratitude more deeply? Can we practice more life-giving kinds of thankfulness? My hunch is that we can. And I am increasingly convinced that we must.

As I puzzled over the problem of "cheap gratitude," a note arrived from a friend. She shared with me how something I had written made a difference in her life, and she thanked me: "For all that you do, I am deeply grateful."

Not just "grateful," but "deeply grateful." She wanted to make sure I knew that hers was not some sort of rote thanks, like a pleasant response one might offer to a sales clerk or a baby-sitter, but that she experienced profound insight and healing and an intense sense of gratitude through the gift my words had provided. Not cheap gratitude, but deep gratitude.

Might that be the problem—that we have substituted a thin veneer of thanks for a radical, transformative experience of wholeness and connection? We fall back on that fragile understanding when what we need is a robust one. We want to give thanks; we appear to be longing for a more rooted experience in the wisdom of gratefulness. But we do not quite know what it is or how deep gratitude might change everything. Having a clearer sense of the nature of gratefulness might be a good place to begin.

GIFT AND RESPONSE

These pages explore gratitude, how to understand thanks and how to practice it. I am not a psychologist or philosopher—the two sorts of experts who have added most to our understanding of gratitude. I write about faith, spirituality, history, and culture—about living purposefully, about how we gather together, and about a world of compassion, care, and love, about faith and God. Gratitude matters deeply to these concerns.

There is no magic fix in these pages, no promise of ten steps to a grateful life. Nor is there a clean, crisp academic definition of gratitude. Instead, I have tried to learn gratitude from the ground of my experience, to pay attention to the cultural and spiritual languages of thanksgiving all around us, and to search for clues and hints of gratefulness in our communal life. As I listened, what emerged surprised me.

I learned that questions and concerns of gratitude surround us all the time. On a personal level, I discovered I am far more thankful than I knew, but that I am often too timid to embrace the full power of gratitude. Not only did gratitude show up when I did not expect it; it also failed to show up when and where it seemed most necessary. On the communal level, it became obvious that there are meaningful and transformative ways of expressing gratitude, and, sadly, there are ways of using gratitude to hurt, abuse, and oppress. In a sense, we live in a dense forest of gratitude. That makes viewing the trees particularly difficult. One can get lost easily.

But if we focus, we can see gratitude more clearly, how it guides us to a way of healing and compassion. With this new vision, we begin to see how it shapes our lives. Once we see, we cannot *un*-see. Gratefulness is not a magic fix, but it just might be the bright star directing us to a new and better place. This book is an invitation to become aware of gratitude in new ways, with the hope that if we see more clearly what is at stake, we might together nurture, encourage, and practice the sort of gratefulness that can change our hearts and our communities.

The first step is to recognize that we carry around in our minds *already existing* structures of meaning that influence how we experience gratitude. For centuries, Westerners have defined gratitude as a commodity of exchange—a transaction of debt and duty—organized around notions of wealth and power. Benefactors gave benefits to beneficiaries who, in turn, were indebted to their benefactors. This debt-and-duty model, built on required reciprocity, is so widespread as to be largely invisible to us, but continually influences us. Yet, as will become increasingly clear in the chapters ahead, this model has not served us well.

There is, however, an alternative structure of gratefulness, one that holds out the possibility of spiritual and ethical transformation—that of *gift and response*. In this mode, gifts exist before benefactors. The universe is a gift. Life is a gift. Air, light, soil, and water are gifts. Friendship, love, sex, and family are gifts. We live on a gifted planet. Everything we need is here, with us. We freely respond to these gifts by choosing a life of mutual care.

Some people think of God as the giver of all gifts; others consider these gifts as part of nature. Whether you believe God or not-God, however, gifts come first. We would not even exist without them. We are all beneficiaries. How we define gifts and givers makes up the deeper structure of our lives.

Gifts bring forth gratitude, and we express our appreciation by passing gifts on to others. When we share gifts, we become benefactors toward the well-being of all. Ultimately, the new structure is a way of being. Although it may be "new" to some in Western societies, this is an ancient understanding, one that echoes through many of the world's oldest and wisest sacred traditions. It is an invitation to receive gifts, live more simply, graciously, and freely, attuned to our own hearts, our neighbors, and the common good. Many of us were taught that it is more blessed to give than to receive, but the truth is that we must first receive in order to give. As a result, we choose to care more freely, fully, and deeply.

In these pages, I argue that gratitude is not a transaction of debt and duty. Rather, gratitude is a spiritual awareness and a social structure of gift and response. Committing ourselves to exorcising the ghosts of the old model and embracing and practicing gift-and-response gratefulness will empower both personal and social change. And it might be what saves us, as individuals and as communities.

A DYNAMIC STRUCTURE

The structure of gift-and-response gratitude is dynamic; that is, it is not like the steel frame of a building. Instead, it is organic, integrative, and internally complex. Because of that, it is particularly hard to see. If quizzed about it, many people define gratitude as a feeling, but that does not take into account deeper dimensions.

At the most basic level, gratitude involves two aspects of experience:

emotions—feelings in response to gifts
ethics—actions in response to gifts

that function in two arenas of our lives:

the personal—the "me" of individual life
the public—the "we" of community

Gratitude involves emotions and ethics, both of which are located in the "me" and the "we." With this in mind, we can create a balanced model of gift-and-response gratitude that looks something like this:

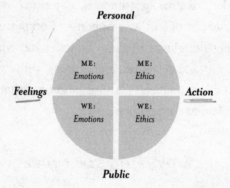

Gratitude is not, of course, a pie chart. Rather, think of this graphic as a round table or a circle. In this way, we can begin to see it as a whole made up of constituent parts working in harmony with one another.

For whatever reason, however, we often fail to experience the connections of the whole. Some of us more easily gravitate to one aspect of gratitude than another. For example:

- If you emphasize *me and emotions,* you are probably attuned to the inner dimensions of awe, surprise, and appreciation and have strong feelings when someone helps you, serves you, or gives you a gift. You define gratitude in terms of delight, joy, or surprise.

- If you emphasize *me and ethics,* you might experience gratitude as a moral or ritual response to a favor extended to you. Returning dinner invitations, writing thank-you notes, and repaying personal obligations come naturally. You think of gratitude in terms of individual responsibility and reciprocity.

- If you emphasize *we and emotions,* gratitude might well up in your heart when you are with others expressing appreciation—singing the national anthem, celebrating the victory of a favorite sports team, worshipping in church or synagogue, or gathering around the family table. You experience gratitude through family, community, and national celebration and festivity.

- If you emphasize *we and ethics,* you might define gratitude as social responsibility that demands action through public commitments to charity, stewardship, volunteerism, and social institutions. You believe that gratitude is an essential foundation of civic life, taking pride in doing good.

Such emphases emerge from our personalities, life experiences, faith traditions, and what we learned in school or from our parents. Most of us lean toward one of these understandings of gratitude more than the others. Yet thinking of gratitude as *only* one aspect of the larger field of thankfulness throws the whole thing off balance. If you emphasize gratefulness as your own feelings, the chart might turn into something like this, a disordered, disconnected, and distorted view of gratitude:

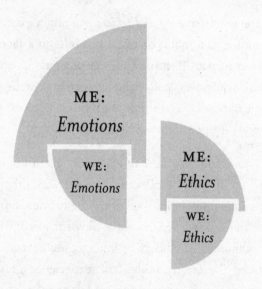

Of course, a different chart can be drawn for each of the different preferences. When we see gratitude this way, the challenge becomes obvious. With diverse understandings of gratitude, we run the risk of not noticing the expectations of other people. And we might not even notice when we are grateful. I have learned that I emphasize *me and emotions,* although I grew up in a *me and ethics* household—one attuned to a strong personal obligation toward benefactors. No wonder I felt bad about gratitude. My family minimized my natural inclination toward grateful emotions in favor of personal duties related to giving thanks. Neither of these forms is bad or good; they are just different. Not surprisingly, because I did not share my family's perspective, I felt like a failure.

In order to develop a mature sense of gratefulness, we need to strengthen all four dimensions and be aware of the connections between them, developing a way of life that attends to our feelings and actions in relation to gifts and does so personally and communally. We need to open our eyes to a fuller vision of gratitude to grow in well-being and live compassionately together.

AN INVITATION

Although it pains me to confess it, I have spent much of my life worried that I was an ingrate. I did not mean to be one. It was not intentional. Gratitude was hard. I did not really understand it. Others misunderstood how I experienced it. I disliked the notion of debt and duty and required reciprocity. I did not choose to be thankless. Mine was a sin of omission, not commission.

Eventually, however, ingratitude caught up with me. I realized I needed to do better, understand more deeply, and trust that a life of thankfulness held out new possibilities for hope, joy, and love. What follows in these pages are not the findings of an expert, but the wonder and surprise of someone who has discovered that—even in midlife—gratefulness can change things. A lot of things. Really surprising things that helped me see my own life, my work, and the world from the perspective of gifts and responsiveness, empowering me with deeper resilience and a more profound sense of compassion for my neighbor's well-being. Gratitude has made me more aware of sacredness and the Spirit, more committed to justice and politics.

Here I share those discoveries, drawn from science, sociology, and spirituality. Gratitude integrates the sciences and faith in surprising and refreshing ways, showing they are not in tension, but together reveal healing dimensions of human experience. When speaking of faith, I draw mostly from Christianity not because I think Christianity is the best, but because that is the tradition I know best. Jesus stood in the great line of Hebrew prophets who said quite a bit about gratitude—most of it radical, political, and transformative. As part of my own journey, I have learned that gratitude is a central theme in the Bible, and that it is also central to all great ethical systems and religions. Giving thanks may well be the primary practice shared by religious—and nonreligious—people. This is not a religion book. Rather, it is a gratitude book that takes faith, the Bible, and theology seriously as an aspect of the grateful life. I hope you have patience with me when I write of Jesus (I think you will find the Jesus in these pages surprising); and I trust you will freely translate my Christian stories into the stories of thanksgiving from your own tradition and life. Gratitude is not the exclusive possession of any single way; rather, it is truly a path that welcomes all.

I have called this chapter a "confession." Making this gratitude confession did not come easily. I also know that confession is spiritually empty without "amendment of life." Confession is a call to do something, to change, to live a different way. Admitting I was at a loss when it came to being thankful led me to learn gratitude afresh, to practice thanks in new ways, and to act on behalf of others with more grace. When I started down this path, it seemed like penance. But then it became a pilgrimage, a journey from "no thanks" to a more grateful life.

If you are eager to experience the transformative power of gratitude, I invite you to join me. Think of this book as a kind of "thanksgiving" table, one set with words. Listen to tales of gifts and grace. Bring your own. You might just find yourself more grateful too.

Inner thoughts of awe,
surprise & appreciation
Gratitude = delight, joy
or surprise

Me: Emotions
Gifts and Thanks

Everything is a gift. The degree to which we
are awake to this truth is a measure of our
gratefulness, and gratefulness is a measure of
our aliveness.

—DAVID STEINDL-RAST

1

Feeling Grateful

Grace and gratitude belong together like
heaven and earth. Grace evokes gratitude like
the voice an echo. Gratitude follows grace
like thunder lightning.[1]

—KARL BARTH

I poked my head out the back door and called: "Rembrandt!
Remmie! Come in! Come in, boy!"

No response. I surveyed the yard.

"Rembrandt, where are you?"

In recent months, the dog had slowed down quite a bit. Age
was taking a toll, as were the seizures that he occasionally suffered. Sometimes I rubbed his back knowingly, "We don't have
much time left, little friend."

"Rembrandt! REMBRANDT?" I called with more urgency.

I walked outside and looked around. He was not there.

Sweat poured from my forehead, panic increasing as my anxiety multiplied in the early morning heat. Memphis forecasters had predicted unusually high temperatures and humidity for the next week. These professionals were used to Southern summers, but even they said it would be bad—dangerous really. "Stay indoors, stay hydrated," they warned. Where was that dog? This weather is bad for him.

Then I saw it: a small opening in the fence off the porch. A decade earlier, I had gotten Rembrandt from a shelter. He had been a runaway. No one came to claim him. When we met, he was little more than a puppy, a black terrier mix of some sort who could have doubled for Toto in *The Wizard of Oz*. He had that same spirit too, ready to jump out of a basket and run down whatever road was before him. He hated confinement—the spirit of escape never left him. He loved to jump, squeeze, explore. I stared at the hole in the fence knowing it had beckoned an elderly canine to adventure. He was gone.

For four of the hottest days in the history of Memphis, we searched for him, around our neighborhood, near the zoo, at Overton Park. We hung up signs, called the shelter. He needed water and food and medicine to survive. I was frantic. I could not imagine my beloved dog dying, starving and alone. Through several difficult years of my own life, including graduate school, losing my job, and getting divorced, Rembrandt had been my most faithful companion. I could not bear to lose him this way. I could not sleep. I could not stop crying.

Someone called us saying she had seen him, taken him in for a day, and fed him before he ran off again. My heart raced: he was still alive! Then another neighbor reached us with news that

Rembrandt had been found stumbling down a street, suffering from dehydration. My husband drove to their house, picked up the dog, and immediately took him to the vet. I stayed home and kept a worried vigil by the front window.

What seemed like hours passed. Finally, the car pulled up. I raced outside, threw the door open, and grabbed Rembrandt from the seat, nearly crushing him in a motherly embrace. His hair was matted and covered with thorns and brambles. He was beat up and exhausted, but that did not matter. His eyes told the truth—he was glad to be home. He nuzzled me and licked my face. What was lost had been found.

"You are home! Home! Never, never, never run away again," I laughed and scolded while tears streaked my cheeks. "Thank you! Thank you! Thank you! Thank you!" I was speaking to the dog, my neighbors, my husband, and God all at the same time. All my feelings of fear and grief were overwhelmed by a far more powerful emotion: gratitude.

GRATITUDE AS EMOTION

At its simplest level, gratitude involves feelings. We *feel* thankful. It is a natural response to certain circumstances. Some event transpires, and we feel grateful for a particular resolution—a good medical test for ourselves or a loved one, missing a collision with an oncoming car, the safe birth of a baby, a new job or financial provision, a child's graduation from high school or admission to a good college, and any number of life's surprises or events. As a feeling, however, gratitude is more complex than, say, happiness or sadness. Gratitude involves a set of emotional responses that merge with certain circumstances to cause us to feel what we experience as gratefulness. When Rembrandt was lost and then found, I felt love for him, fear over his loss and perhaps death, relief at his being found, appreciation toward neighbors and my husband, and the gladness of reunion. To share this story on social media would require a string of emoticons, as no single "face" would capture the full sense of gratitude.

Many experiences of gratitude combine love, anxiety, relief, and gladness, but others do not. You might feel thankful that it did not rain during your beach weekend. Those are feelings of appreciation and enjoyment. Feeling grateful for a new job might be caused by the fact that your last job was so awful that you could not bear it another minute—you might be thankful to have escaped! Over the years, I have known people to experience intense gratitude after leaving abusive relationships or bad marriages. Those are feelings of release and moving on.

Gratitude often pairs with achievement and reward. Work well done, a long project completed, an idea carried through: these are all episodes of resolution and satisfaction that result in genuine thankfulness. Spending time in nature feeling connected with the world often elicits gratitude. A sunrise might make us happy for the miracle of a new day; a mountain vista can call forth a sense of awe that moves the soul toward thanksgiving. Seeing a beautiful painting, attending a concert, or reading a well-written novel brings forth feelings of appreciation for the talent of the artist or author and a sense of amazement at having received a gift from a stranger. Even though these situations differ widely, they all elicit something we call gratitude.

So what *is* gratitude? In each of the previous examples, it becomes easy to see three things that are true about feeling grateful. First, the *situation matters*. Whether an event engenders positive or negative emotions depends on the situation. Changing jobs can sometimes cause stress instead of elation and anticipation, completing a project might bring sadness rather than joy, a mountain might be an obstacle to climb rather than an inspiring vista, and writing a paper might just be an onerous class assignment instead of a welcome challenge.

Second, the *emotions* that weave into gratitude *range widely*, from relief, appreciation, and release to surprise, wonder or awe, and gladness and joy. Third, it is typically an *unplanned response*. We do not calculate it. Feeling thankful naturally arises from our experiences as we go through life. Together, these three elements reveal that gratitude involves recognizing a circumstance, event, or situation is a gift of some sort—something that we benefit from, that surprises us, and that we could not plan—and we have a strong emotional response to it. Ultimately, gifts elicit gratitude. We like gifts. We respond to gifts.

I cannot think of gifts without thinking of Christmas. Over the years, people have given me gifts I have forgotten, gifts I have treasured, gifts I did not particularly appreciate, and gifts that brought forth deep gratitude. On Christmas morning in 2016, my daughter pulled a large box from under the tree and placed it in front of me.

"Go ahead," she said, with a hint of excitement. "Open it, please."

Off came the paper and the lid, and inside the big box were five smaller packages. Each one had been carefully wrapped, and each bore a message that twinned with gifts of chocolate, tea, and coffee. When read together, each gift contributed to a larger message: "Times are 'dark' [for dark chocolate], so we need someone who is 'counterculture' [a coffee] and full of 'wisdom' [a tea] to preserve the 'longevity' [a tea again] of the 'world' [another chocolate]." She knew that the recent presidential election had upset me—and she knew that I was working on a book that I hoped would make a difference. She did not simply give me things I liked from the grocery store. Her gift to me that morning was encouragement.

Looking at the box, with all its thoughtfully created packages, wrapped with such care, I knew that she—my young-adult daughter—believed in me. I had not always been certain she understood my work. But she did, perhaps even more than I knew. Small tears of joy formed. I managed to choke out, "Thank you." She reached toward me, I reached back, and we hugged. No gift was more urgently needed or so meaningful. There was no lost dog on that day, no worry or fear of loss or illness, just that holiday ritual of Christmas gifts. Yet her gift of "I believe in you" gave rise to surprise, delight, appreciation, and courage—a most welcome emotional experience of gratitude.

And that is what is odd about gratitude—it is rarely the same from one incident to another, and few experiences of gratitude are exactly like other experiences. Dog: fear, anxiety, grief, hope, relief. Christmas: wonder, surprise, delight, appreciation, encouragement. Both resulted in something called gratitude, but they were entirely different. Situations change, and the emotions vary. Not only do they differ from each other in our own lives, but they also differ from person to person. There is no one experience of gratitude; rather, it is a complex and episodic thing, and one that is deeply personal.

In spite of that, most of us can relate to the dog and holiday stories, as we recognize some similar experience and set of emotions in our own lives. If we all shared our stories of thanks, our words would no doubt invoke memories of gratitude in others. For all its uniqueness and complexity, there is a common core to feeling grateful: we recognize a circumstance, event, or situation (even if it is a trial) as a gift, we have received some unexpected benefit, we respond with words and actions, and we become our best selves in the process. Gifts are not only pleasurable, but the right gift at the right time can change us. When such gifts arrive, we know it. Something deep within rises to the surface, that mixture of love and appreciation we call thanks.

AN EMOTION—OR AN EXCHANGE?

And then there is the office holiday gift exchange, where everyone spends a limited dollar amount on a generic gift to be exchanged for another generic gift from a co-worker they may or may not like. Participation is required. Everybody must bring a gift to swap for another. The gifts are obligatory. People do not generally express deep gratitude for these presents. Indeed, the gift cards, coffee mugs, and boxes of candy are usually forgettable—and sometimes annoying or even insulting. But if someone gives you a gift, you have to give one back. That is the way it works.

The idea of gift exchange is quite ancient. For eons, gratitude has been understood as an obligation to repay a favor or gift. It was defined as an exchange between a benefactor and a beneficiary. Gratitude can be formulated in this way: A (benefactor) gives B (gift) to C (beneficiary), and C gives D (a favor, token, or duty) in return to A. This equation proceeds along in a line but then arcs back to the giver in a one-direction balance of benefit:

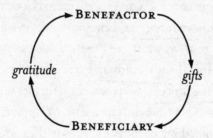

This is known as reciprocity, "the norm of" the idea of doing something in return for the person who does something for you.[2] It was a moral obligation, to use an old-fashioned term, "a bounden duty." Reciprocal gratitude operated in the spheres of politics, society, and the practice of virtue.[3] Ancient philosophers like Aristotle and Seneca speculated upon it, exploring gratitude as a divine virtue and communal necessity. To do something in return for a gift reflects appreciation for the giver and is the proper response to a benefit. Ingratitude—the failure to respond—was considered a violation of social norms. Only those ill-formed in virtue would neglect to express gratitude in a tangible way.

But this system of gifting and gratitude, this quid pro quo (Latin, literally, "something for something"), was also used as a means of patronage, power, and control: "I do something for you, so that you *must* do something for me." A gift incurred a debt, and the recipient owed a response—an act of gratitude—in return. Within this framework, ingratitude was more than bad manners. Returning the favor was a duty, a requirement. Gratitude consisted of far more than personal obligation. It served as a foundation of society. Benefactors and beneficiaries existed in binding relationships built on benefits.

The emperor or king gave his subjects the "gifts" of protection and provision. In return, subjects offered loyalty, homage, service, tithes, and taxes. If you failed to return the ruler's favor—such as not paying a tribute or refusing to send your son to serve in the army—you were branded an "ingrate." Ingratitude was disloyalty and sometimes treason, crimes punishable by denial of favor, reduction in rank, seizure of property, enslavement, prison, exile, or death. Most pre-capitalist societies practiced this quid pro quo sort of gratitude, with its complex of gifts given, debts incurred, and favors owed. In it limited benefits flowed down from privileged benefactors to regular people; and most of the wealth flowed up from subject beneficiaries in the form of "gratitude" to those at the top. Gratitude was not a feeling. It was the law.

Modern Western societies inherited these notions and practices. Gratitude was important and central to civic life, but Europeans also struggled with unjust and unequal structures that privileged benefactors to the detriment of beneficiaries. In the 1700s, philosophers like John Locke argued that public life and politics should be separated from gratitude. Civic relations should be based on rules and laws—not gifts, favors, or quid pro quo—with the participation and consent of the governed. Private life, philosophers suggested, could still be ordered by gifts and gratitude in the more limited arenas of families and friends. Thus, constitutions eventually replaced kingly rulers, and laws distributed political benefits through the will of the people.

Gratitude did not disappear, however. It was exiled to the private sphere, where, as one historian notes, it became "a soft virtue reserved to drawing rooms, dance halls, romances, and novels of manners." Gratitude, he says, became a "sentiment."[4] Thus, gratitude assumed the language of emotion. In the domestic realm, reciprocal rules of gifts still mattered and benefactors still had to be honored, but feelings became increasingly important. As a result, gratitude came to be seen as a "feminine" virtue, something soft and sentimental that occurred mostly in the realms of neighborliness, friendship, social duty, courtship, and marriage.

Most of the gratitude books on my desk make this emotive point visually—their covers are pastel, often illustrated with flowers, with titles written in flowing fonts. The impact is one of coziness, holding forth a promise primarily for women who inhabit the domestic world. Gratitude has been "feminized." I deeply distrust the language of "feminization," as it often signals—especially among academics—a realm of "less than." When something is feminized, it loses its intellectual bite and is relegated to "mere" feelings.[5] A few contemporary intellectuals are trying to reclaim the importance of gratitude, but some of that work seems to dismiss the emotional dimensions of gratefulness altogether. To take gratitude seriously, they say, we must push feelings aside.

This is odd considering the derivation of the word "gratitude." The word *gratia*, meaning "favor, regard, pleasing quality, goodwill," is the Latin translation of the Greek word *kharis*. Kharis was the name of one of the three goddesses, collectively called the Kharites (the Three Graces), who bestowed the gifts of charity, beauty, joy, festivity, and song. The Kharites were indiscriminate givers and embodied gratitude and benevolence in the ancient world. Kharis, who personified both giving and beauty, was sometimes conflated with Aphrodite, the goddess of love. Thus, even in ancient societies, it was a mistake to reduce gratitude solely to the virtue of political exchange. Gratitude was not an obligation or duty. Rather, its origin suggests gratitude arises primarily in our hearts, with a sort of wildly unpredictable pleasure attending it.

Classics professor David Kosten picks up this understanding from Aristotle (who held conflicting opinions about gratitude), insisting that the philosopher included gratitude in his discussion of emotions by saying that one could "have gratitude." He writes: "'To have *kharis*' means one thing and one thing only in classical Greek, and that is to feel gratitude."[6]

Thus, gratitude as a feeling is neither sentimental nor soft. Although gift giving might have been appropriated by ancient rulers to enhance their wealth and power, gratitude was originally seen as part of the divine feminine, a kind of gratuitous distribution of joy, wonder, provision, and creativity—all entwined with love and beauty. Indeed, Kosten further argues that gratitude was "first and foremost an emotion, or *pathos*," that it is a feeling in response to a favor done for the sake of others with "no self-interested motive on the part of the benefactor."[7] Gratitude, in this mythic sense, was the human response to gifts with no strings attached, no repayment expected. In Western culture, the move of gratitude from the throne room to the drawing room may have actually (and ironically) preserved the truest nature of thankfulness as a feeling—or a complex of feelings—related to love.

The right place to begin understanding gratitude is as an emotion issuing from the heart, that pulsing, mysterious place at the center of our being. The heart is not a place of clear definition or philosophical precision. The heart hides from the analytical gaze. We hear and feel its beat but barely understand its work-ings. I suspect that when most people consider gratitude, they think of it as a feeling issuing from the heart. Of those 78 percent of Americans who responded to the survey question, "Have you *felt* [emphasis mine] a strong sense of gratitude in the last week?" I am sure not one answered, "Yes. This past week, I entered into a reciprocal relationship of social exchange and indebtedness." Instead, I am sure the reply was, "Yes. This week, I *felt* grateful."

INDISCRIMINATE GIFTS

The closest things we have in Western societies to a celebration of the Kharites are the festivals of indiscriminate gift giving: Christmas, Hanukkah, winter solstice, and the secular winter celebrations. I am a practicing Christian, and I have always loved Christmas, especially its religious aspects. When I was a girl, one of my favorite parts of the season was unpacking and setting up the manger scene—with all its figures of the holy family, the animals, shepherds, angels, and wise men. I felt kin-ship with the lovely, lithe Mary, dressed in blue and pink. But I was also fascinated by the wise men, those mysterious kings from the East. I did not know entirely what to make of them—their black and brown faces forming a compelling counterpoint to those of our white baby Jesus and his mother. The wise men wore regal robes and carried exotic gifts—gold, frankincense, and myrrh—to an infant born to peasants in a barn.

I understood one thing, however. There was no way that Je-sus and his family could ever repay the debt of gratitude owed by receiving these presents. Nothing would—nothing could—be given in return. The manger scene was not a gift exchange.

What must Mary and Joseph have thought? What insanity was this? They, good Jews, subjects of Roman oppression, did not receive gifts from kings. Indeed, kings took from them—their freedom, hope, dignity, livelihood, land, and taxes. Maybe the whole business of gifts from the Magi made them a little afraid. The New Testament says that Mary "treasured," not the gifts, but these confusing things and "pondered them in her heart" (Luke 2:19). No word of Joseph's response, however. I wonder if he might have wanted to give the loot back for fear there were strings attached.

The story of the three kings is not only a pretty tale; it is a pretty radical one. It inverts how we think of gifts. Typically, peasants offered a gift to a king to demonstrate loyalty or request a favor. But when kings bring gifts to peasants, it turns what we think of gifts and giving on its head. It is not the case of a poor baby's parents pleading or making good with some wealthy benefactor. The baby did nothing to deserve the gifts and cannot repay any debt of gratitude. This giving of gifts reverses the normal order of things, showing not the power of kings, but the undoing of the benefactors' status and entitlement. What wonder! What surprise! Obligation is gone, replaced by complete astonishment. Repayment is neither possible nor necessary. Gifts are truly gifts, not debts to be discharged. The relief might make our hearts fill with the surprise of kind tenderness, the ache of thanks. The baby, the star, and the wise men: a story of gifts and radical gratitude. Joy to the world!

"DON'T GIVE ME ANYTHING"

Social scientists, unlike political philosophers, insist that gratitude is a "blended emotion" that includes "awe, admiration, reverence, envy, resentment, embarrassment, and jealousy," but that it is ultimately a "tender emotion."[8] Researchers have discovered that it is actually harder for men than women to feel grateful—or admit when they do feel it. Especially American men. Perhaps this has to do with the history of gratitude and its being consigned to the domestic sphere during the Enlightenment. Men worked in the public world of rules and policies, whereas women inhabited the private sphere, where feelings and practices of gratitude were retained. Eventually, this fueled a gender divide in the area of gratitude. In the 1980s and 1990s, a series of studies detected "gender-role stereotype traits" associated with gratitude, in which men found it more difficult to be grateful because of "judgments about debt and dependency" and expectations of male self-reliance. In one such study, some men found gratitude to "be a humiliating emotion" that is best concealed.[9]

A distaste for indebtedness and a preference for independence, readily admitted by the men in these studies, act as stumbling blocks to gratitude. Although these studies focus on men, the factors they bring to light may apply to some women as well. If one sees self-sufficiency and individualism as highly valuable traits, feeling grateful can be perceived as uncomfortable, weak, and perhaps demeaning.

Such feelings, while more common to men, are not unique to them. My grandmother, for example, left school early to help feed her family during the Depression, got pregnant as an unwed teenager, and struggled with a son who was both mentally ill and a criminal sexual predator. She was tough and worked hard. When she was a girl, she had dreams of becoming a teacher, but she was poor and her local public school did not go past eighth grade. In exchange for an education, some Catholic sisters asked her to scrub floors at a local convent that ran a high school. She took up the offer. It was a genuine quid pro quo arrangement—they would teach her, and in payment she would clean for them. But when she wound up pregnant, the sisters sent her packing. She never became a teacher, and she never trusted promises like that again.

In many ways, she succeeded in life—she had a surprisingly stable marriage, enjoyed a long career with a major retail company, and nurtured her other children in relatively good ways. She too loved Christmas, mostly because she loved giving gifts. But she hated getting them. She would always say, "Don't give me anything. I don't want or need anything. And if I do, I can get it myself." These were the words of a scrappy working-class fighter—a woman who had known poverty—and charity—and never wanted to be indebted to anyone again.

She embodied the spirit of philosopher Ralph Waldo Emerson's observation from 1844: "It is not the office of a man to receive gifts. How dare you give them? We wish to be self-sustained. We do not quite forgive a giver."[10] To my grandmother, self-sufficiency was the whole point of life. Achieving that was freedom. She wanted to get and stay ahead. She was fiercely proud. Gratitude was not in her playbook.

A few years before she died, she had a religious conversion. After the debacle with the sisters, she did not, as far as I know, practice much of any religion. When she neared sixty, however, she developed heart problems, stopped working, and found herself dependent on my mother. This did not suit her, of course, and things got very hard. Then she started reading the Bible, began talking about Jesus, and joined a small Baptist church with a quirky and kind preacher who believed in the power of salvation. It made a difference. It changed her.

On occasion, I would go to church with her. She loved the sermons. She loved Bible study. But she really loved the hymns—especially "Amazing Grace," a hymn she had never sung until she joined that little church:

> *Amazing grace! How sweet the sound*
> *that saved a wretch like me!*
> *I once was lost, but now am found;*
> *was blind, but now I see.*
>
> *'Twas grace that taught my heart to fear,*
> *and grace my fears relieved;*
> *how precious did that grace appear*
> *the hour I first believed.*
>
> *Through many dangers, toils, and snares,*
> *I have already come;*
> *'tis grace hath brought me safe thus far,*
> *and grace will lead me home.*

Although a well-known and beloved hymn, when my grandmother sang it, it was as if it was brand-new, uniquely her story, and tears often accompanied its verses. "Grace," she would say with great dignity, "Grace. That's the whole story. That's everything."

She lived a few more years, not easy ones. In the long process of dying, she had realized that life was a gift and that even her hard-won victories came, in part, through the love and goodness of others. I never heard her say, "I'm grateful," but I know she was thankful every day she was alive during those last years, for the people she had known, for the loves she had, for the beauty of her beloved adopted state of Arizona, for blue skies and sun. She had a great capacity to laugh, to see deeply, and to embrace the poor, strangers, the "little guy," and outcasts. The tiny Baptist church reminded her of God's love and the gifts that surrounded her. There she learned a deep spiritual truth: none of us is truly independent. We need each other, the earth, and (for her as well as for many others) God. And the thread of that interdependence is grace.

The words "gratitude" and "grace" come from the same root word, *gratia* in Latin and *kharis* in Greek, as mentioned earlier. In addition to being the name of a goddess, "grace" is a theological word, one with profound spiritual meaning. Grace means "unmerited favor." When I think of grace, I particularly like the image of God tossing gifts around—a sort of indiscriminate giver of sustenance, joy, love, and pleasure. Grace—gifts given without being earned and with no expectation of return—is, as the old hymn says, amazing. Because you can neither earn nor pay back the gift, your heart fills with gratitude. And the power of that emotion transforms the way you see the world and experience life. Grace begets gratitude, which, in turn, widens our hearts toward greater goodness and love. Thankfulness is a feeling in response to gifts.

Together grace and gratitude form a different moral "equation." The standard model of gratitude is a closed cycle of gift and return bound by social obligation and indebtedness, whereby a "benefactor," a superior of some sort (someone wealthier, more powerful), provides a benefit for another, a "beneficiary," a person in a state of need or trouble. In the closed cycle, the beneficiary is *dependent* on the benefactor in a way that feels demeaning or signals indebtedness—and that was surely the objection of the men in that study. This is why my grandmother found gratitude humiliating. No wonder. Few want to be on the receiving end of an unequal transaction.

Although we might chafe at the idea, there is nothing inherently wrong with recognizing our dependence—maybe a better term is "mutual reliance." To be human is to rely on others. All of us are dependent every day upon general gifts given, like food we receive from the soil and the farmers who grow it, to more specific ones, like lunch a friend buys for you when you forgot your wallet. We should appreciate the work and kindness of others in taking care of our needs. We rely on one another, each other's work, and our shared stewardship of the earth and its resources. It is good to be thankful for these things. If we take the time to recognize mutual reliance, we feel appreciation in a positive, pleasing way. The problem arises when benefactors use their position to control others—and to benefit only themselves—through their benefactions.

If we change a closed system to an open one, banishing transaction and substituting grace, the picture of gratitude shifts. In the closed cycle of debt and duty, the roles of benefactor and beneficiary are static, and gifts are commodities of exchange, based in transaction and control. It feels awful to be stuck in such a system. Indeed, the philosopher Thomas Hobbes once referred to this as "thraldom." But in an open cycle of gratitude, gifts are not commodities. Gifts are the nature of the universe itself, given by God or the natural order. Grace reminds us that every good thing is a gift—that somehow the rising of the sun and being alive are indiscriminate daily offerings to us—and then we understand that all benefactors are also beneficiaries and all beneficiaries can be benefactors. All that we have was gifted to all of us. There would be no benefactors if they were not first the recipients of grace. In other words, gifts come before givers. We do not really give gifts. We recognize gifts, we receive them, and we pass them on. We all rely on these gifts. We all share them.

This is not a fulfillment of duty or a single act of kindness, but an infinite process of awareness and responsive action. The gift structure of the universe is that of an interdependent community of nature and neighbor that extends through the ages in which we care for what was handed to us and give gifts to others as a response. This is not a closed circle of exchange; it is more like the circles that ripple across a pond when pebbles are tossed into the water. Everything is a gift.

In a small way, Rembrandt's story exemplified all of this. Finding a lost dog is almost always a communal effort, from strangers enlisted to look out for your beloved pet, to the neighbor who takes him in, to someone determined to discover a dog's true owner. During that hot Memphis week, my family— and my little dog—were utterly dependent on the kindness of others. But that dependence revealed something else: the interdependence of our neighborhood, the surprising care of people whose names we never knew, and the shared emotional experience of loving a dog. Each person in the unfolding of events that led to Rembrandt's homecoming gave a gift of some sort, and together they became a circle of goodness. Not only was I grateful that Rembrandt was found. I was grateful for my neighbors and a neighborhood that cared, people I discovered I could— and did—depend upon.

Gratitude is complicated. Feelings of dependence—and interdependence—can be both elusive and resisted, mostly because they are caught up with soul-crushing ideas of obligation and debt. But if gratitude is mutual reliance upon (instead of payback for) shared gifts, we awaken to a profound awareness of our interdependence. Dependence may enslave the soul, but interdependence frees us. More than two centuries ago, German theologian Friedrich Schleiermacher referred to this experience as the "feeling of absolute dependence." To him, absolute dependence was not demeaning. It was more like what we describe today as interdependence. He recognized that gratitude was the truest state of reality—everything exists in an infinite relationship of gifts to everything else—and it was also the starting place for a life of meaning, as our own awareness opens toward others, the world, and, ultimately, God.

2

Heart Matters

Piglet noticed that even though he had a Very
Small Heart, it could hold a rather large amount
of Gratitude.

—A. A. MILNE

The gifts were piled under the Christmas tree. Some of the packages for our young daughter were marked: "To Emma, from Mommy and Daddy." But a certain number of gifts bore a different tag: "To Emma, from Santa." Emma chose to open "mommy and daddy" gifts first, for which she happily (yet dutifully) thanked us. She saved the Santa presents. They were special. She greeted each with a squeal of delight, amazed that some mysterious stranger from the North Pole had provided such largess on Christmas morning. Sitting in the midst of boxes and torn wrapping paper, she looked up and, with just a hint of confusion, asked, "Why does Santa give me so much? I can't even say thank you!"

Gratitude to a particular giver is known as "targeted gratitude." We know who gave the gift, as when my daughter thanked us for her Christmas gifts, and we can respond to the giver appropriately, whether with a reply, a note, or some other acknowledgment of the gift. This is the territory of saying thank you to parents or grandparents, acknowledging volunteers on a project, or bringing a gift to the host of a party. In all these instances, there are clear benefactors, benefits, and beneficiaries, and all participants enact their particular roles in the exchange. This is what scholars call "the norm of reciprocity." One knows whom to thank. Knowing from whom a gift comes surfaces an array of emotions from appreciation to humility and feelings of dependence and the obligations of debt.

Benefactors may be people we know, like our parents, or those we do not. Indeed, after I graduated from college, I found myself unable to pay my rent. The situation was dire, and I asked friends to pray for me. One afternoon, when I picked up the mail, there was a letter addressed to me—with no return sender—and inside was a cashier's check from a local bank for that month's rent payment. I felt the way my daughter would so many years later: "I can't even say thank you!" By removing him- or herself from the equation, that benefactor did not want me to experience any of the awkwardness of obligation. But there *was* a benefactor, even if unknown to me, I was the beneficiary, and the benefit was deeply appreciated. It was a targeted gift. I appreciated the kindness and provision, and my immediate needs were met.

A second kind of gratitude, referred to as "untargeted gratitude," relates to the field of grace rather than the exchange of benefit. This form is "the emotional state of feeling grateful when there is no one to thank." Untargeted gratitude is usually related to life and health, unexpected good luck, or awe and wonder—experiences like cuddling a newborn baby, finding a twenty-dollar bill on a sidewalk, or seeing a dazzling sunset.[1] Some ethicists contend that this sort of thankfulness, where no giver is involved and no reciprocal gesture can be made, is a lesser form of gratitude. Others, however, insist that untargeted gratitude creates an emotional desire to "pay it forward" rather than simply to repay a giver.[2]

In the past, mostly because we could only imagine gratitude as a closed circle, we often turned "untargeted gratitude" toward a specific target: God. A century ago, if you survived an epidemic, God had spared you. If you found a bag of silver under a tree, God had directed you to find it. If you saw a breathtaking sky, God had given that vision to you personally. Many of our ancestors believed that God had specifically given a gift to them, an act of divine provision, in a direct and magical fashion, like a box under the Christmas tree with their name on it, signed, "From God."

And the response? Thank you, God! Say a prayer. Do a good deed for someone else as a demonstration of thanks. Donate money for a new stained-glass window in the church. No gratitude could ever be diffuse or "untargeted" in that universe. God was the Heavenly Benefactor, the One who gave you everything you needed and only wanted your thanks in return.

This raises a host of questions, however. Why were you saved from the epidemic and not your children? What about the person who lost the bag of silver and now cannot pay the rent? What if the sky brought forth tornadoes? Did God send the storm to destroy your village? And what about next time? If God does not heal you or pay your bills or the sky is gray? Does that mean God is withholding gifts? That you are being punished? That you did not say thank you enough last time, and now God is mad? Making God a personal benefactor in these cases creates difficult questions about God—questions that cause many thoughtful people to reject all notions of God, if not providence altogether.

In the New Testament, there is an interesting verse about gratitude: "Every generous act of giving, with every perfect gift, is from above, coming down from the Father of lights, with whom there is no variation or shadow due to change" (James 1:17). At first glance, this verse might seem to make God the ultimate benefactor. But this is not about targeted gift giving from God, who is handing out goodies and wants thank-you notes in return. Instead, "every" gift and "every" act of giving is a reflection of the light—the most diffuse of all divine metaphors!—shed upon the whole world, a light that shines everywhere, all the time, accessible to all. The emphasis is on that which is untargeted, not the divine benefactor.

These words echo Jesus's claim that the sun rises and the rain falls on the "righteous and the unrighteous" (Matt. 5:45). Yes, the New Testament records some specific, targeted miracles. But far more often, Jesus speaks of a wildly untargeting God— one who lavishes drunken wedding guests with even more and finer wine, who throws seed around with abandon, who issues invitations to the unnamed poor to dine, who throws a party for a profligate son, and who multiplies fish and bread so that thousands might eat not once but twice. On a massive crowd relentlessly pursuing him, he showers blessings: "Blessed are the poor! Blessed are those who hunger!" (Matt. 5:3, 6). Standing up on an ancient hill, Jesus yells out: "Presents for everyone!"

These gifts are not targeted. They simply are. They are not obligations to be repaid; rather, they are gifts to be enjoyed. There are no expectations of exchange. No transaction involved. The author of James goes on to say that if you understand *in your heart* that gifts and gratitude are part of the very fabric of the universe, you will both be a better person and do good in the world (1:19–27). This is all-encompassing grace.

Targeted gratitude, with known givers, and untargeted gratitude, arising from profligate gifts, reflect the emotional complexity of thankfulness. Gifts may come "tagged." In that case, we appreciate particular givers and may feel happy and humble. Other gifts may come without tags, and those typically move us toward mystery, awe, and wonder. You might think of God not as a Heavenly Benefactor, but as the Indiscriminate Giver. Or, if you are not a theist, perhaps nature itself, with all of its gifts, calls forth your untargeted gratitude. Or you respond to the gifts of human culture, learning, and science. Whatever the case, we are all un-targets of gifts that surprise and sustain us. Untargeted gratitude takes us out of the cycle of obligation into the larger circle of shared gifts, beyond reciprocal exchange toward mutual enjoyment and responsibility for those gifts. Opening our hearts to the constant flow of receiving and responding that happens all around us all the time makes us more generous.

A GRATEFUL HEART

The seat of gratitude is the heart. Yet the workings of our hearts remain, in many ways, mysterious. On December 28, 2016, celebrated Hollywood actor Debbie Reynolds died at age eighty-four. The previous day, her sixty-year-old daughter, Carrie Fisher, star of the *Star Wars* films and noted author, had unexpectedly passed away from complications following a heart attack. A headline in the *New York Times* asked: "Did Debbie Reynolds Die of a Broken Heart?"[3] And that is a real thing: stress-induced cardiomyopathy, known as "broken heart syndrome," when people who are particularly close die within a short time of one another. Indeed, that happened to my great-great-grandparents. Married for almost sixty years at a time when few people lived so long, they passed away within an hour of each other. Broken heart syndrome.

Of course, we may never know about Debbie Reynolds. Nor does the death certificate for my great-great-grandparents say "broken heart." But the heart is a complex organ, necessary to all of life and susceptible to injury of both body and soul. We human beings did not always understand its biological functions, but somehow we came to celebrate the heart as the seat of emotions, conflating biological existence with the feelings that make our lives both miserable and glorious.

During the last two decades, researchers have discovered real links between the heart and gratitude. Even before I was paying close attention to the subject of gratitude, snippets of these findings made their way into my field of view—an article in *O* magazine, a conversation on daytime television, an interview on NPR. Most of the popular discussion claimed that negative feelings like anger and fear could not coexist in the same space with positive ones like happiness and gratitude. Robert Emmons, one of the world's leading researchers on the subject of gratitude, summarizes this research from studies on heart patients:

"Gratitude drives out toxic emotions of resentment, anger, and envy, and may be associated with better long-term emotional and physical health in transplant recipients."[4]

Indeed, multiple studies demonstrate connections between well-being (life satisfaction and happiness), physical health, and gratitude. In heart patients who are asymptomatic, researchers found that people who were grateful slept better, were less depressed and tired, and were more self-aware and confident, with lower risks of inflammation. According to one study, gratitude is a dimension of "spirituality and/or religious wellness"; it suggests that gratitude interventions might lower the risk of heart disease.[5] "It seems that a more grateful heart," says researcher Paul Mills, "is indeed a more healthy heart."[6] Other studies show that gratitude promotes regular heart rhythms, rebalances hormones, reduces stress, increases relaxation, and promotes resistance to common illnesses.[7]

In addition to heart health, gratitude has also been linked to emotional well-being, lower levels of anxiety and depression, decreased panic attacks and phobias, reduced risk of alcoholism and substance abuse, and longevity (yes, grateful people live longer). Researchers found that thankful people live happier lives as well—they are more attentive to pleasure, experience less envy, are more contented, and retain good memories of the past easily.[8] Robert Emmons summarizes gratitude benefits as increased self-esteem, enhanced willpower, stronger relationships, deeper spirituality, boosted creativity, improved athletic and academic performance, and "having a unique ability to heal, energize, and change lives."[9] The link between gratitude and the heart is so pronounced, one research team identified gratefulness as a "strength of the heart."[10]

As I read the scientific literature on gratitude, I thought back over my family's history. The generations before me had, with only a few notable exceptions, been plagued by depression, obesity, substance abuse, and heart problems. Certainly, these problems can be genetic in nature. But I also wondered if we were plagued by a gratitude deficit, a kind of hereditary ungratefulness. My mother lost her sense of gratitude as death came closer, and my grandmother struggled with gratitude in relation to poverty. Who knew how many generations had failed at thankfulness? Health, psychological, and economic problems might have numbed our ancestors to feelings of gratitude; ingratitude might have worsened the originating issues and added more to the mix. This may have caused limited economic and personal success, which then resulted in cycles of mental illness, abuse, and poverty. In turn, those problems set up the next generation for more struggle and undermined their children's possibilities for gratefulness. My family had been on a downward spiral for a long time. Was learned ingratitude part of the puzzle?

An awareness of my own family history began to dawn on me—and how it might relate to my own struggles to feel grateful. But in spite of these realizations, I felt worse. The literature seemed to taunt me. If only I were more grateful, all these good things—health and happiness—would come my way. But I just did not *feel* it. Not in the way that the studies suggested I should. I wanted my heart to sing with gratitude, but it was just so damn hard. None of it was natural to me. Did being born into a cycle of ingratitude consign me to a life without thanks, a heart straining toward an elusive grace?

It can be hard to feel what you have not been taught to feel.

TURNING THE TRAIN AROUND

As a teenager, I became friends with a few high-school class-mates who attended Scottsdale Bible Church. My mother was horrified at the time, calling them "Bible thumpers" and "fundamentalists." I just thought they were nice. They did not call themselves by any particular label, although "Bible-believing" was probably the most common way they referred to themselves. And, as it seemed to me at the time, they took the Bible and the spiritual life more seriously than did my parents' Methodist church. So, hungry to know God, I broke with my family's long-standing tradition and opted to go to church with my new friends.

Their world was intriguing to a fifteen-year-old seeker. Mostly, as I recall, they loved charts, and many of them hung on sanctuary walls and mapped the Bible in an attempt to make the mysteries of Christianity as clear as possible. In this universe of lines and arrows, where faith was diagrammed like the complex sentences of grammar class, nothing stood out to me as much as this little train:

It was odd in some ways that people who urged one another to be born again and invite Jesus into their hearts would arrange life in this way. To them, the Bible taught the facts of salvation (not the feelings of such), and faith was a response to these facts. Feelings came last, if at all. Indeed, the youth pastor explained, "A train still works without a caboose, but it always needs an engine." Yes, a youth minister told a roomful of teenagers to bury their feelings. "Emotions aren't important," he went on, "They come and go. God's truth is all that matters. And that has nothing to do with your feelings."[11]

I stared at that little fundamentalist train, and every fiber of my Methodist soul inwardly shouted, "NO! Feelings are important!" John Wesley, the founder of my family's religious tradition, had said exactly the opposite—faith sprang from an encounter with God in which the heart felt "strangely warmed." From a renewed heart came faith, and then our vision of the world changed—in effect, the "facts" of existence (including the "fact" of God) were apprehended with emotional awareness, a spiritual sense that could interpret life and purpose through love. The youth pastor had reversed the Methodist train.

I looked around the room. Everyone else was nodding in agreement. Following their lead—and as the diagram asserted—I said nothing and went along with the group. After all, the pastor had been to seminary. I was a newcomer. Maybe I had misunderstood John Wesley. Certainly all these Bible Christians knew better than I did. Eventually, I learned that they believed only certain emotions were acceptable, and some feelings were downright dangerous. But happiness, submission, pleasant agreement, assurance, and conviction were all welcome. Good feelings proved that one was faithful in following God's truth. Negative feelings indicated that the faith train was going off the rails (or perhaps that Satan was driving your train). Emotions must be held in careful check to theological orthodoxy, the "facts" of the

Bible. This embrace of a narrow range of "right emotions" was something I would later call orthopathy (from the Greek *ortho*, "upright, right," and *pathos*, "feeling").

Although my fundamentalist friends had clearly defined feelings as "less than," most white American Protestants (and many white Catholics as well) also live in religious cultures of emotional constraint. My Methodist parents spoke of Wesley's strangely warmed heart as part of history, but our Methodist church embodied that snarky moniker "God's frozen chosen," the style of Protestantism in which decorum and order are prized above other aspects. In white churches, expressive faith has been left mostly to Pentecostals, but those communities also theologically police emotions so as not to let things get too out of hand. Thus, gratitude as a feeling is not something easily grasped by even many religious Americans; gratitude is mostly appreciation in announcements or thank-you notes or through singing hymns.

Many white churches also seem to teach gratitude as transaction, a quid pro quo of faith. God loves us, so we must love God back, and if we do not, God sends us to hell. This is a deeply inadequate view of gratitude—one that diminishes its power as a complex emotional aspect of life. Salvation is just one more transaction in a closed cycle of gratitude.

The truth is that we usually *feel* something when we receive a gift or when we encounter grace. Awe, appreciation, surprise, humility—these are things of the soul that speak of our deepest needs and longings. These feelings should be neither constrained nor consigned to life's caboose. They need to be acknowledged, embraced, and celebrated. In the United States, historically black churches have gotten this better, with expressive music and a rich theological language of blessing, where thankfulness flows as a balm in sermons and worship, creating a spiritual environment that, in effect, teaches people to *feel* abundance in the face of oppression, injustice, and (often) deprivation as a way to better know God and oneself.

In non-European religious communities, the emotions of gratitude serve as the foundation of personal resilience and joy, as a soulful pathway to the truest kinds of freedom and liberation. Gratitude can be experienced by anyone, anywhere, without permission and without restraint. No external master can either release or inhibit thanksgiving. Gratitude is, perhaps, the most immediate and most primal of all spiritual affections—one that makes every human being a priest. Feeling grateful empowers the soul.

I did not grow up in a black church. I grew up in a bunch of white ones. Maybe racial privilege blinded us to gratitude. After all, we deserved good things and success. The American dream was ours. God gave it to us. Saying thank you was polite recognition of that fact. Maybe saying thank you too profusely, however, made us feel humiliated that we were not as in control as we thought we were. Maybe that emotion made us a little bit mad, or scared when gratefulness pushed against the boundaries of authority and orthodoxy. But there, in church, like pretty much everywhere else in my life, feeling gratitude too deeply was a bit like a guest who overstayed her welcome.

I am not a psychologist. But, over the years, I have learned that emotions—whether positive or negative—do not behave very well when ignored or pushed aside. A good life, including healthy spirituality, incorporates the wide range of human emotions relating to each other in ways that make each of us unique and open us to a sense of purpose and meaning. Maturity is act-ing in a manner consistent with our inner reality, integrating feelings with intellect and integrity. Maturity is being fearless in face of emotions and owning up to feelings denied or derided.

Emotions do not tell us that climate change exists or who the president of Zimbabwe is. They are not "facts" in the way that scientific or historical data are. But feelings are the data that point toward our inner realities. Feelings alert us to what is unresolved in our lives, what is missing in our hearts, the brokenness that needs mending, and the relationships that need tending. When we do not feel grateful, something is blocking the feelings—and whether that something is learned or feared is important to explore.

SUFFERING AND ABUSE

About two hours outside of Lexington, Kentucky, on a narrow country road sits a small Baptist church. It embodies the spirit of rural America as much as a church can—a white clapboard building surrounded by fields and woods, with mountains in the hazy distance. A cemetery sits on the property too, holding saints in the peaceful earth as they await resurrection.

I have been to all fifty states in America, including Kentucky, but I have never been to this particular church. I have seen it on-line, but I do not ever want to visit in person. Somewhere in that graveyard, resting among the Baptist faithful, lay the remains of the uncle who abused me when I was fourteen years old. When my mother sent me an e-mail in January 2007 telling me he was dead, I replied, "Thank God." It was the first time that any men-tion of my uncle and any word of gratitude were ever combined in a sentence. Once in a while, I look at the graveyard from the safe distance of the Google cam—wanting, I think, to reassure myself that he remains in the dirt.

Researchers say that negative emotions—fear, envy, greed, entitlement, resentment, anger, and regret—block gratitude, causing "self-alienation," broken relationships, and profound unhappiness, thus resulting in a worldview that is "deeply false to human nature and the nature of the universe, a distortion of reality."[12] Indeed, it hardly takes a doctorate in psychology to know that what Christians refer to as the seven deadly sins— really, seven deadly emotions—run counter to thanksgiving and get one to a wretched place of existence if left spiritually unchecked. At the same time, "grateful people tend to be satisfied with what they have" and are less likely to succumb to negative emotions.[13] It is a bit of a therapeutic and theological gerbil wheel: positive people are grateful, and grateful people are positive; negative people are ingrates, and ingrates sink into a mire of maladjustment. The trick, according to this analysis, seems to be ridding yourself of your negative emotions.

It is one thing to explore a family history of negative emotions, and it is a necessary part of maturity to take responsibility for the hurt you choose to embrace or the bad feelings you cultivate in your own life. But what if negative emotions stem from real sources and are not of your own doing, not your own fault? What if you fear not because of the prospect of losing what you have or never getting what you desire, but because your uncle used to invade your bedroom at night? What if you are angry because you have been violated and no one protected you? What if you regret the loss of your sense of personhood and safety or resent that your life was interrupted by a sociopath? These are not just "negative" emotions. They are important feelings induced by trauma, violence, and abuse, and they are natural human responses to pain inflicted upon you. It would be much worse if a victim did *not* feel fear, anger, regret, and resentment.

Negative emotions are not always our fault. Even so-called negative emotions like envy and greed have complex origins. An acquaintance shared with me a story of being bullied. When he was a boy growing up in west Texas, he thought he might be gay. Evidently so did his classmates, who harassed him ruthlessly for being a "sissy" and "pansy." At night, while crying himself to sleep, he would vow, "I'll show them. I'll be smarter and richer than all of them! Then they can't hurt me!" It became his emotional mantra. He worked hard, put himself through college, left rural Texas, and became a successful investment banker. When still in his thirties, he bought a dream house in a posh California coastal town.

"You know what I felt?" he asked. "Not grateful. I was mad that I didn't have a view of the beach. Some people might say that it was envy. But I was always the little boy trying to protect myself from the bullies. I never felt safe." He said with a sigh, "It took me a long time to learn gratitude."

For some people, gratitude can be very difficult. A classmate from my days at an evangelical college had a poster hanging—of all places—above the toilet in her bathroom. It depicted a cheerful garden and was emblazoned with words from the New Testament book of 1 Thessalonians (5:16–18):

> Rejoice always,
> pray without ceasing,
> give thanks in all circumstances;

for this is the will of God
in Christ Jesus for you.

Honestly, I always wanted to rip it off the wall. I was secretly full of fury at injustice, not only the injustice I had suffered, but the larger agonies and evils endured by people less fortunate than even my own sorry self. But I knew that such an emotional insurrection would lead her to believe that Satan had possessed me—and it would result in all sorts of gossipy prayers for my salvation. So there it remained, taunting me like one of Job's tormenters every time I had to relieve myself.

"It is worth noting," write the authors of one gratitude study, in typically detached academic jargon, "that while gratitude is considered a positive psychological factor, it is not necessarily good for all people under all circumstances, e.g., displaced gratitude under conditions of exploitation."[14] No kidding. Put that on a poster, girlfriend. Telling victims to be grateful for trauma, violence, or abuse only wounds those who have suffered and empowers perpetrators. Gratitude may work miracles, but sometimes the miracle comes from just being able to feel anything but pain. Feeling thankful might just have to wait. Gratitude cannot and should never be forced or faked, and it is never appropriate to cover up or deny abuse or excuse injustice. Indeed, gratitude as a placebo can be another form of abuse that silences those in deep pain with false notions of forgiveness, happiness, and well-being.

Emotions drive our lives—not from the back of a train, but often as the engine. Negative emotions and positive ones. Our lives are an intricate mix of feelings created through myriad circumstances, many of which are beyond our control. Some of our problems with feelings occur when we cannot embrace what is just there, when we judge or fear our own emotions. One of the most helpful teachings in Buddhism is the idea that suffering simply exists and that it is intensified by human refusal to acknowledge the reality of pain. Suffering actually increases when we resist, deny, or fear negative emotions; those emotions often cause shame; and shame blocks gratitude. As human beings, part of our job is to be able to recognize what causes pain, to work toward healing, and to learn how to live in the world with empathy, forgiveness, and gratitude. Embracing our humanness, with its mixture of sadness and joy, fosters vulnerability and authenticity and takes us toward maturity and deep love. "Gratitude," writes Catholic theologian and justice activist Mary Jo Leddy, "does not dispel the mystery of suffering and evil in the world and may even deepen it."[15]

It is not easy to live with the mysteries of pain, injustice, illness, and violence. We humans rightly rage against these indignities, those things that work against joy, love, and peace. For decades, I wrestled with shame and hatred regarding my uncle. Those emotions were exacerbated by other incidents where I was rejected, hurt, or felt violated. The negative feelings were powerful, sometimes driving the train to what felt like the edge of an emotional cliff. Gratitude does not take that away. Gratefulness is no panacea against violence and injustice. Yet my soul suspected there might be a path beyond rage—a way for gratitude to enfold the pain in a greater good. These words from the Catholic spiritual writer Henri Nouwen spoke to me:

> To be grateful for the good things that happen in our lives is easy, but to be grateful for all of our lives—the good as well as the bad, the moments of joy as well

as the moments of sorrow, the successes as well as the failures, the rewards as well as the rejections—that requires hard spiritual work. Still, we are only truly grateful people when we can say thank you to all that has brought us to the present moment. As long as we keep dividing our lives between events and people we would like to remember and those we would rather forget, we cannot claim the fullness of our beings as a gift of God to be grateful for.[16]

Along the way, a friend, a person who herself had known suffering, said to me, "Your life is like a garden, and it is not well tended. You need to grow your garden." Until then, I had never really thought of the emotional life as a garden—an organic metaphor—but that is much closer to reality. Our emotional lives are like gardens. Experiences are akin to soil, the rich *terroir* in which our feelings grow. Left untended, certain emotions can choke out others, like the wild grasses that threaten my lettuces every spring. There is nothing inherently wrong with weeds—it is just that they get in the way of dinner! So I pay attention. I know the difference between the seedlings I plant and the invasive ones, cultivating the greens and pulling out what would make my family sick. So it is with our emotional lives. The same soil allows both weeds and desirable plants to grow, and it takes a watchful gardener—and more than a little practice—to ensure the health and productivity of the whole. I learned to work the garden and discovered that it was the spiritual work of gratitude.

In a very real way, suffering is just the soil. From it grow both negative and positive emotions. The negative ones are like weeds in the high summer, the positive ones—including gratitude—too often the smallest of shoots. Over the years, I have discovered that hard work on one's knees is the surest way to tend the garden. Both in prayer and in rooting around in the dirt of the soul, I recognize the difference between what is fruitful and what will inhibit the growth of goodness and then pluck out the invasive species. But, if the work is done, the garden flourishes. And there gratitude grows.

I cannot remember a single moment when I was able to forgive. It did not work like that. Instead, I went on tending the garden, growing what could be grown and rooting out the weeds. Then, one morning some forty years after the fact, I woke up feeling sorry for my uncle. I thought about how he had gone to prison, how my aunt divorced him for "emotional cruelty." I remembered how the pastor who buried him begged my mother to pay for a grave marker. She refused. I wondered what had wounded him so, why he had made the choices he made, and perhaps who had hurt him that he hurt others. What happened long before I was born? Had he been a victim too? I felt something. Pity? Empathy? I do not know. But I saw him as a deeply flawed human being, not a monster, a person who had wasted his life, who had squandered the only real gift he had, lived bereft of hope and love, and lies in an unmarked grave.

And I felt oddly grateful. Not for his suffering or for the injustice done to me. No one should ever feel grateful for sin, evil, or violence. No one should ever express gratitude for the bad choices of others—those bad choices are never gifts. I do not know if what I felt was forgiveness, but I experienced a profound sense of appreciation that my own pain had not taken the same form that his had. This suddenly seemed a miracle, as was the awareness that my life has been, for the most part, rewarding. A good family, strong faith, meaningful work—all the things that had eluded him. Somehow, I had found courage and conviction to make it through and in midlife could say thank you to those around me, to the universe, to God.

Gratitude had grown in that soil, good soil. It was not the dirt of shame. All the shit had only enriched the dirt. Somewhere, in the earth, thanksgiving had taken root. From the ground had sprung life. Through seeding and weeding, the vine had come forth, and its fruit had ripened.

For that, my heart felt grateful.

THE GIFT

As an emotion, gratitude can be elusive—so easily blocked by regret, loss, anger, and fear. So I tried to keep a daily record of gratitude. When I did, however, I realized something important. I was filling the little yellow diary with things: a pleasant meal with my family, a surprise compliment, a new book contract, a car repair, my daughter's grades at college. My gratitude diary became a kind of list of the benefits of being a middle-class white person. It actually made me uncomfortable. I realized that I thought of gratitude as a commodity tally, a sort of positive emotional account of nice stuff. To pay attention to good things was a helpful practice, as it displaced negative attitudes related to entitlement and privilege—things that often blocked my ability to see my own life clearly. However, the diary missed what was revealed in my long struggle with abuse, and what was most important.

Gratitude, at its deepest and perhaps most transformative level, is not warm feelings about what we have. Instead, gratitude is the deep ability to embrace the gift of who we are, *that we are*, that in the multibillion-year history of the universe each one of us has been born, can love, grows in awareness, and has a story. Life is the gift. When that mystery fills our hearts, it overwhelms us and a deep river of emotions flows forth—feelings we barely knew we were capable of holding.

At that moment, we might feel stunned. We might thank God. We might thank our ancestors and the random choices they made that created the line that led to us. Mom and dad, the big bang, evolution, whatever. But we might also feel the transcendent awe of life, that in the entirety of the cosmos, through the enormity of time, I am, you are, we all are. What we feel when we contemplate that, that feeling is gratitude.

"Life is the first gift," said poet Marge Piercy, "love is the second, and understanding the third."[17] The *first* gift is life. My life. Your life. There exists a unique beauty and dignity at the core of each one of us, the quality that animates every human being and that Jews and Christians call "the image of God." That is the gift. No other gift is possible without it. Nothing we ever receive or have can rival it. Gratitude is not about stuff. Gratitude is the emotional response to the surprise of our very existence, to sensing that inner light and realizing the astonishing sacred, social, and scientific events that brought each one of us into being. We cry out like the psalmist, "I am fearfully and wonderfully made!" (Ps. 139:14). When we push aside the immediate anxieties of that existence, we can actually see more clearly that to feel fear, doubt, or anger at all is part of the gift of life itself. Without life, even the negative emotions are impossible. Everything else is dependent on that one thing. All we experience is radically contingent on a single gift—life.

Few have understood this as thoroughly as Elie Wiesel, Holocaust survivor and novelist, as here in an interview with Oprah Winfrey, herself an abuse survivor:

> OPRAH: There may be no better person than you to speak about living with gratitude. Despite all the tragedy you've witnessed, do you still have a place inside you for gratefulness?
>
> ELIE: Absolutely. Right after the war, I went around telling people, "Thank you just for living, for being human." And to this day, the words that come most frequently from my lips are, "Thank you." When a person doesn't have gratitude, something is missing in his or her humanity. A person can almost be defined by his or her attitude toward gratitude.
>
> OPRAH: Does having seen the worst of humanity make you more grateful for ordinary occurrences?
>
> ELIE: For me, every hour is grace. And I feel gratitude in my heart each time I can meet someone and look at his or her smile.[18]

This insight stands out: *When people lack gratitude, "something is missing in their humanity." People can "almost be defined by their attitude toward gratitude."* Wiesel is not speaking of appreciating material goods. He means that our ability to experience life as a gift, to treasure that gift, and to feel its power, even in the most violent and demeaning of circumstances, is the very essence of human existence. Life is the gift. Not what we have, but that we are.

To feel gratitude is not the caboose of some faith train. It is the beginning. To feel appreciative awareness of our own lives—and feel that awareness of the lives of all those around us—is rather like being reborn, as we look at ourselves, our experiences, and the world with eyes of surprise and wonder. Pay attention to those who have suffered and who found gratefulness. Listen to the voices and songs of the marginalized, the thanksgivings of those who have been abused and oppressed. Embrace the sorrows of your own heart. These are the teachers of gratitude. Do not be afraid.

"Is there a word that captures the characteristics of a grateful person?" asked psychologist Philip Watkins. In the midst of data points and research citations in his academic textbook, a startling statement appears. "I believe there is a word that helps answer the question," he opined. "For me, that word is *grace*; grateful people are full of grace."[19] Grateful people feel life to be a gift.

"Every hour is grace," said Elie Wiesel. Yes, an amazing grace. And a gift.

II

Me: Ethics
Awareness and Practice

"Thank you" is the best prayer that anyone
could say. I say that one a lot. Thank you
expresses extreme gratitude, humility,
understanding.

—ALICE WALKER

3

Habits of Gratitude

Gratitude unlocks the fullness of life. . . .
It makes sense of our past, brings peace for
today, and creates a vision for tomorrow.

—MELODIE BEATTIE

The sign outside read "Trinity," and a stylized dove hovered above the logo formed from a Celtic cross and triangle. Underneath the picture, the line read, "Assemblies of God." I wandered into the small church on my own, no friend, no family to accompany me. I was only seventeen, following the path of life's first spiritual journey, and I had no idea that the Assemblies of God was a Pentecostal denomination, a group emphasizing the power of God through gifts like speaking in tongues and miraculous healing. I was not looking for any of that, however. I was just curious about church.

The sanctuary was simple, more like a cafeteria with carpet and nice chairs than any traditional church. Although the building was new, the congregation was not small—many people filled the seats as a professional-sounding band played music to warm up the crowd. The preacher, in a business suit, an odd choice of vestment for an Arizona summer, stood up.

"Welcome!" he shouted, "Welcome to God's house! Let's all thank Jesus for bringing us here! Get up! Stand up! Thank Jesus!"

The music swelled and people swayed, some chanting in a language that sounded like Latin to me, but full of strange intonations, maybe Chinese. The pastor pointed at a woman in the congregation.

"What do you thank Jesus for today?" And the reply: "That my mother was healed!" He shouted back, "Praise Jesus!"

He pointed again, "And you?" The response was tearful: "God paid my electric bill!" "Yes!" cried the preacher, "Thank you, Jesus!"

The music went on—a soft-rock litany of "Thank you, Jesus, thank you, thank you, Jesus."

"Oh yes!" the pastor shouted, now needing no prompt from the congregation. "Thank you, Jesus! We all thank you! We praise you and thank you!"

It was like a spiritual sea, full of waves of praise, as all around me people with eyes half open joined their words to his as if mesmerized by gratitude, first gently whispering thanks and then shouting praise. From every direction flowed thanks—appreciation for miracles received, prayers answered, healings bestowed, financial provision, good weather, missionaries in foreign lands, heathens converted, children who spoke in tongues, the pastor's recent sermon, and all who came to paint the new church. Hands were raised, palms facing up, waiting to receive the gifts of a good God; lips were ready with eager words of thanks. Everyone awaited grace, overwhelmed by gratitude.

Everyone except me, of course. I felt nothing.

Well, that is not entirely true. I was bewildered by this polyphony of appreciation. Maybe a bit angry, as I felt left out of their thanksgivings. My teenage prayers were not being answered. I had not been healed (I struggled with migraine headaches). I did not share their secret praise language (it would be nice to be special). I was not rich (quite the contrary), was not popular (the main woe of being seventeen), had no boyfriend, wondered about love, sex, and college, and feared the rapture, the end-times, and the war of Armageddon. I had nothing but a pile of teenage worries and fears, heightened by reading the book of Revelation and *The Late Great Planet Earth*, a scary paperback I had bought at the local grocery store. All these happy people proclaiming the good things God had done for them—all this thanks—made me dizzy. The room seemed sweaty with gratefulness.

Then the pastor started pointing at people in my section. "What are you thankful for? And you?"

Thankful? I was terrified he might ask me.

I slipped out of my seat and headed for the door. When I reached the car, with its Jesus bumper sticker, an icon of my newfound faith, I breathed and sighed, "Thanks, Jesus. For getting me out of there. Thank you."

An Ethic of Thanks

It might have been the first time I felt like a stranger in a room of thanksgiving, but it would not be the last time I ran away when called upon to render thanks. That, of course, is the problem with gratitude as a feeling. We resist feelings. We might not be feeling the same thing everyone else is. Or, as in my case, gratitude might only show up once we have escaped to the parking lot.

Emotions are random things. Love, sadness, joy, fear. Very few are predictable, and most move like winds through our lives. They depend on what we have eaten or how long we have slept, long-term problems and immediate circumstances. I suspect that is why my evangelical friends put "feelings" at the end of their faith train. Emotions are ephemeral. Feeling is great when you feel good, but what about when you do not? Or when your feelings run counter to those of everyone else in the room?

Gratitude is like other emotions. Thankfulness might sneak up by surprise, but it cannot be planned. Yet gratitude is good. Think of all the benefits that scientists report: health, happiness, and well-being. So the question arises: How do you experience gratitude when feelings are elusive?

Part of the answer lies in the nature of gratitude itself. It cannot be overstated that gratitude is an *emotion,* a complex set of feelings involving appreciation, humility, wonder, and interdependence. Gratitude is, however, more than just an emotion. It is also a disposition that can be chosen and cultivated, an outlook toward life that manifests itself in actions—it is an *ethic.* By "ethic," I mean a framework of principles by which we live more fully in the world. This ethic involves developing habits and practices of gratefulness that change us for the better. Gratitude involves not only what we feel, but also what we do.

In this way, gratitude resembles love. Love is also a complex set of feelings—desire, passion, devotion, and affection. We *feel* love. But love is also a commitment, a choice, and a vow, an emotional orientation toward a person or persons that causes us to act in certain ways. Love as a noun, a feeling, surprises us; it shows up and changes everything. As most of us know, however, it is also a bit of a cheat. It can disappoint, fade, or taunt when it seems to hide or move away. Love as a noun can be tricky. When it is, we choose, often motivated by the memory of the feelings, to love and act accordingly. Love moves from being a noun—an emotion we feel—to a verb—an ethic of commitment we embrace. Gratitude is like that. Some amount of the time we feel grateful, but when the emotions seem to desert us or show up at all the wrong times and in the wrong places, we can choose to give thanks and act in accordance with grace. Gratitude is both a noun and a verb. Gratitude is both a feeling and a choice. The first often arises unannounced and the second takes a lifetime of practice.

To compare love and gratitude underscores one of the most important things about gratefulness—it is ultimately about connection. Most typically, we feel grateful when someone does something for us. We discover that we are, in some way, unable to meet our own needs. That may make us feel humble, but it should also inspire us to act in return. Not only should we say thank you to the benefactor; we should reach out toward other people in need. To live gratefully involves a number of skills: noticing when a kindness is done or a benefit is received; returning the gift of thanks to the giver or embrace the sense of awe instilled; and sharing benefits with others as we are able. Like love, gratitude multiplies through giving and receiving. Both love and gratitude can become far more than ephemeral emotions—with practice, they become habits. More than anything else, love and gratitude take time to learn, understand, and develop. Only in this process can we experience deep gratitude.

Cultivating Awareness

How does gratitude move from feelings to a disposition of character, from an emotion to an ethic? Perhaps the first task is to be aware of blessings. Brother David Steindl-Rast, a Benedictine monk noted for a lifetime of gratitude practice, has observed: "Ninety-nine percent of the time we have an opportunity to be grateful for something. We just don't notice it. We go through our days in a daze."[1]

Being in a "daze" is essentially living on autopilot. We follow habitual paths of emotions and actions, the familiar routines and rituals that make up our daily existence. "All our life," claimed psychologist William James in 1892, "so far as it has definite form, is but a mass of habits—practical, emotional, and intellectual— systematically organized for our weal or woe, and bearing us irresistibly toward our destiny, whatever the latter may be."[2]

One of the most helpful books I have read in recent years is Charles Duhigg's *The Power of Habit*. In it, he explores the findings of neuroscience showing how much of our activity is habitual—based in a cycle of cues, routines, and rewards that form the well-worn brain pathways of daily existence.[3] These are simple things like your morning ritual of waking up, getting out of bed, drinking coffee, checking your smart phone, and seeing that your favorite team won the game (or not). We do not think about these things. We just do them, as William James would say, "semi-mechanically, or with hardly any consciousness at all."[4]

For many of us, gratitude is not a habit. We have few cues to initiate routines of gratefulness and do not regularly experience its rewards. Many people are far more cued into habits of frustration—like when a car cuts them off on a morning commute or an opinion expressed offends them, which results in the "reward" of feeling superior or in control—or habits of anger, sadness, or cynicism. It seems we have more cultural tendencies toward these habits of woe than toward those James calls habits of "weal," or well-being.

Thus, developing cues to actually initiate thankfulness and establish a routine is a way to foster gratitude. Most gratitude books and websites urge readers to do things like keep a daily gratitude journal, write thank-you letters to important people in their lives, meditate, pray with gratitude beads, create rituals of thanksgiving, and do good things for others in need. But they also recommend establishing "cues"—like "when you wake up," "before a meal," "last thing at night," or "on Sunday afternoon." Cues remind us to look for blessings (awareness) at particular times or places, engage in routine gratitude activities (actions) in relation to those cues, and notice how we experience positive emotions that result (rewards). Social scientists and medical professionals call these *gratitude interventions*, replacing negative habits that cause emotional harm with more positive ones. Such interventions have been found to increase health and well-being among patients with a wide variety of physical and mental illnesses. The use of these techniques is becoming more widespread by those interested in personal spirituality and by professionals seeking good outcomes for clients and patients.

But there is a downside to these findings. The interventions are often part of short-term studies, and even experts acknowledge that we do not yet have clear evidence about the success of gratitude techniques for the longer term.[5] Can interventions turn into long-term habits, routine pathways of grace?

As I read about the benefits of gratitude, I kept thinking about the problems associated with losing weight. Most people can maintain a weight-loss routine for a month, maybe three or six. As long as they stay on such a diet, they lose weight. As soon as the routine ends, however, many people regain the weight. Good diets, however, are not short-term routines. Instead, a good diet introduces people to more nutritious food, exercise, and emotional balance—it stops being merely a diet and becomes a new way of life. A good diet changes one's life, yet making the shift from a quick fix to the long-term habit of healthy eating is surprisingly hard. It seems that gratitude interventions may be similar—successful as long as you keep the journal or remember to write the letters, but as soon as those end, it is easy to go back to the old pattern. How do we sustain awareness over the long term? Is it possible to become a more aware person? Can thanksgiving become a habit?

AN ACCIDENTAL HABIT

My first job out of graduate school was teaching theology and church history at a small Christian college in Santa Barbara, California. It was not a happy experience. Although my credentials and qualifications were strong, the community expected a certain kind of conformity in regard to doctrine and personal piety that discomforted me. For four years (and in the midst of a divorce), I struggled not only with conflicting expectations of who they wanted me to be and who I was—but also with a hostile tenure committee.

After a lengthy process of evaluation, the president called me to his office.

"I'm sorry," he said. "I'm going to have to let you go."

"Why?" I asked.

"Your work is wonderful. You are an excellent teacher," he assured me. "But you just don't fit here."

He looked at me sadly and then continued with a kind of patriarchal assurance, "You just don't fit. This wouldn't be a good place for you. One day you will thank me for this."

Thank him? I wanted to throttle him. In less than two months, I would be without a job and a paycheck, with few prospects for work in a weak academic job market. Being grateful to the person who put me in this position was the last thing in my mind.

A week later, I was telling a friend about the exchange at that final meeting. "Can you imagine the nerve of him? That one day I'll *thank* him? What kind of nonsense is that?"

I expected my friend to rush to my defense. Instead, he leaned back in his chair and quietly said, "You know, he's right."

"WHAT?"

"Years ago," he continued, "I lost a job. It was painful, and I was angry. It didn't seem like a favor. But eventually it was the event that made me understand that I was an alcoholic. And that led me to get sober. Eventually, I understood that it was what I needed for my life to change. Not that it was easy."

I looked at him. "I'm not an alcoholic. That's not the problem here."

"I get that," he said. "But we all need to look at ourselves more honestly. To figure out who we are and where we are really heading. To correct course. Sometimes that only happens in circumstances like this. One day, I bet you will thank him."

"Did you? Thank the guy who fired you?"

"Yes," he replied, "I did. But not at first. Mostly I wanted to throw him off a cliff. But yes, I did thank him. Years later. After I learned gratitude."

"You can learn gratitude?" I asked. "Isn't it just a feeling? How do you do that?"

"Tell me one thing you are thankful for. Just one."

I struggled. I could think of about a hundred things that frightened and worried me. Finally, I blurted out, "For my friend Julie."

"And that's the beginning," he replied. "Think of one thing each day. Do that. Just one. Write it down in a journal."

Journaling sounded beneficial, so for three years I kept a daily journal as a general practice. At the beginning, most of the journal was complaint. But I followed my friend's advice and remembered to write down one blessing each day, no matter what. It was not easy. As the months unfolded, however, the balance began to shift. Sometimes, there were two or three blessings to write down, and then more. There were days of outright surprise and joy, appreciation for simple pleasures, for the kindness of others, for the richness of life. One such entry stands out for me:

> I went out with J. and told her about two things, about winning the dissertation prize and about that meeting where none of my colleagues would speak to me. She said, "You know, Diana, I've never seen

anything like your life. People hand you a bouquet of roses in one hand and a bag of manure in the other."

Funny enough, I hadn't really noticed that. I was so excited about the roses that I had barely thought twice about the cruelty. Maybe it does make a difference to pay more attention to the flowers than the crap.

I wrote about the painful events connected with losing my first job and the divorce. But I also wrote about good things: beautiful California days, meals with friends, music at a favorite jazz club, sitting at the beach, writing poetry, receiving professional praise and recognition. As the months unfolded, the tone changed from mostly desperation to mostly delight. A larger narrative emerged: what had begun as a period of difficult personal crisis wound up being a time of profound happiness, deepened courage, and new self-awareness.

When my friend suggested writing down what I was thankful for, he suggested an activity that, as I mentioned, is known as a gratitude intervention in the health-care community. Now, as evidence mounts that journaling about blessings (instead of challenges) reduces stress and improves moods,[6] psychologists and medical professionals suggest that patients keep gratitude diaries. Indeed, keeping a gratitude journal is one of the most often recommended ways for people to learn gratefulness, and several popular books attest to its power. Although I did not start out to specifically keep a gratitude journal, the act of journal writing itself (along with my friend's mandate for one blessing a day) became a cue to notice the good things in my life. Putting those things on a page became a routine. As the pages added up, day after day, I literally started seeing my life and the world differently. Over time, this habit became a lifeline for me—as I wrote, I knew that I grew stronger, and I developed a clarity of purpose and experienced more joy.

This process was not a magic bullet, like a twenty-one-day diet promising perfect health. I did not begin journaling and discover that all my problems had gone away. Journaling was not a technique for happiness; instead, over three years, I developed a sustained practice that shifted my perspective. I learned to see differently and, as a result, acted in ways that were more forgiving, just, and hopeful. In the process, I learned two important things: first, when you look for things to be grateful for, you find them; and, second, once you start looking, you discover that gratitude begets more gratitude. Like all habits, gratitude builds on itself.

Gratitude is not only the emotional response to random experiences, but even in the darkest times of life, gratitude waits to be seen, recognized, and acted upon more thoughtfully and with a sense of purpose. Gratitude is a feeling, but it is also more than that. And it is much more than a spiritual technique to achieve peace of mind or prosperity. Gratitude is a habit of awareness that reshapes our self-understanding and the moral choices we make in the world. In short, gratitude is an ethic, a coherent set of principles and practices related to grace, gifts, and giving that can guide our lives.

FROM TECHNIQUE TO PRACTICE

Techniques are practical methods of accomplishing a task, some of which are better than others. We learn all sorts of techniques as we go through life. There are techniques for reading and studying, doing math, driving, managing money, raising children, making meals, maintaining commitments, and caring for our physical or emotional lives. Human beings use techniques to make tasks easier and allow us to accomplish work in—at least somewhat—organized ways. A healthy person learns these techniques from parents, at school, or in a religious community. Most of us, however, do not become experts at the techniques in all areas—we are not simultaneously a teacher, mathematician, investment banker, child psychologist, five-star chef, or our own personal doctor. Techniques provide us with a basic level of capabilities to function in life with a modicum of success.

Practices take us more deeply in a particular activity. For example, when I was a girl, my mother taught me how to cook—how to shop for food, read recipes, and prepare ingredients, how to boil, fry, and bake. She gave me a set of techniques that enabled me to make meals and feed myself and, later on, a family. But I also enjoyed cooking. So I read cookbooks, watched cooking shows, and took over the kitchen with culinary experiments. Soon my kitchen skills outstripped my mother's. I moved from knowing a few basic techniques to being a confident and skilled home cook. I learned how to prepare food in interesting ways, how to combine surprising flavors and spices, and how to work with ingredients I had not known in my childhood. I practiced cooking, and it became an important part of my life, something that gives me joy—and I taught my daughter the same. Cooking together introduced our family to gardening, farmers' markets, issues of food justice, and environmentalism. I will never open a restaurant or win *Top Chef*, but I am a good cook. Techniques are what we use to make do and survive; practices move us to who we become and how we thrive.

Not every technique we learn will turn into a practice, but some will. So it is with gratitude. Most of us did not completely fail at learning the basic techniques of gratitude. Even if we struggled with writing thank-you notes to our grandparents, many of us learned common courtesies, like saying thank you to someone who holds a door or serves us in a restaurant or bringing a small gift of appreciation to a dinner party, as well as ways of celebrating Thanksgiving Day or donating a thank offering in a religious community. Such small acts make life more pleasant and connect us to others as we recognize daily considerations or gifts. We know enough of gratitude to function. But the techniques of thankfulness also hint at something else: that gratitude might be more than a set of skills, something we do on occasion. It can become a good habit. If we practice gratefulness, it becomes a natural and normal way of engaging the world. With gratitude, our hearts open toward one another. It can make us different and help us prosper. The habit can shape who we are.

PAST, PRESENT, FUTURE

Practice takes time. But that is not the only relationship between time and gratitude. When gratitude becomes a habit of being, our capacity to see time—past, present, and future—actually changes. Not only does gratitude open hearts; it also gives us new perspectives on our own lives. It stretches through our experiences—past, present, and future—creating a fabric of appreciation and awareness that forms the story of our lives. When we are thankful for the blessings of what was and see the goodness of what is, what can be comes into view with greater hope and possibility.

Filmmaker Sian-Pierre Regis learned this firsthand. The son of a hardworking single mother, he never appreciated how much she had sacrificed for him. "I was so mean to my mom growing up about having no money," he confessed. When she was fired from her job at age seventy-five, she became depressed. Sian-Pierre wanted to help. He asked her for her "bucket list," the list of everything she had ever dreamed of doing but never could. Belatedly showing his gratitude, correcting himself "for his thanklessness," the son gifted his mother with of all the adventures on her list—milking a cow, taking a hip-hop lesson, flying to her native England to visit her sister's grave, walking the Boston Marathon route. His mother rallied, saying: "I've never felt younger, I've never felt more loved."

Through gratitude, he saw the past differently ("What was I doing? What an idiot," he admitted), she experienced new hope for the future ("I'm excited about going and seeing the next chapter," she said), and together they found a deeper love in the present.[7] Reframing their relationship through gratefulness changed them.

Past, or Hindsight: Gratitude is affected by memory. In some cases, gratitude may be blocked by the memory of negative events. Unable to let the past go, we might be caught up in anger or fear, stuck in events that limit the ability both to feel grateful and to develop the moral capacity of gratitude. In one experiment, researchers discovered that negative memories actually fostered negative moods, while positive memories elevated moods.[8] As Sian-Pierre learned, recalling the past through the eyes of thankfulness strengthened gratitude in the present. Remembering episodes that gave rise to thanksgiving is a good way to reflect on the long story of your life. Gratitude cannot change the past, but it can help us understand the past in ways that give joy and help us flourish.

Oddly enough, most of us have something called "positive recall bias." We tend to remember good things more than we remember bad things. We look backward with rose-tinted glasses, seeing the past as better than it actually was. This is not always a good thing, however, because it can become mere nostalgia. Although it might be pleasant to indulge in nostalgia while at a reunion with your high-school friends, nostalgia draws unrealistic pictures of the past. It makes us believe the old days were always better and what happened in the past is always preferable to the present and the future, that life's only blessings are long gone and we can only be grateful for what was.

So, although we need to recall episodes of gratitude from the past, such memories need to be balanced and honest. We need to remember when gratitude arose from failures, not just successes. For Sian-Pierre, that was the challenge of being poor and needing to see that in a new way. For me, it was when the college president said to me, "One day you will thank me for this." He was essentially telling me that in the future I would recall that awful moment and realize it was the source of new strength and purpose, a bad episode would result in gratitude.

That is exactly what happened. Now, twenty-five years later, I think, "What would have happened if I had stayed in that job?" There may have been benefits, but I would have been stuck in a place that limited me intellectually and religiously, ultimately a dead-end. Freed from that particular job, however unjust it felt, I found my life opened up to people, places, ideas, and experiences that could otherwise never have happened. I learned new things about myself, about God, about life—all of it possible only because I was fired. I feel thankful.

Honest hindsight does not foster nostalgia. It puts us in touch with gratitude. Looking back offers the opportunity to rewrite our own stories in more constructive and positive ways. Sian-Pierre took a story of poverty and turned it into a story of abundance. I took a story of anger and turned it into a story of discovery. In both cases, a hurtful past is redeemed through a new perspective. Can you remember an event that was painful at the time, but that now makes you feel grateful? I suspect most of us can. When we think back, a contrast emerges between immediate loss and eventual blessing. This creates a new vision of our personal history, and "this contrast is fertile ground for gratefulness."[9] Remembering the actual past—even if that past was difficult and filled with ingratitude—allows us to see the past from an angle impossible at the time and paves the way for fuller appreciation of present joys.

Present, or Wide Sight: A few years ago, I was being interviewed about a book I had recently written. The interviewer, a deeply spiritual woman, commented, "You have soft eyes. This entire book is an exercise in soft eyes."

I felt a little panicked because I did not know what she meant.

Seeing my distress, she continued, "The capacity to see widely, to view the whole picture."

I nodded. We went on.

As soon as I got back to my hotel room, I did an Internet search of "soft eyes." Sometimes called "wide-angle seeing," the term comes from the martial arts and refers to awareness that reaches toward the periphery, the edge of what we usually see. The Quaker spiritual writer Parker Palmer describes it this way:

> In the Japanese art of Aikido there is a practice called "soft eyes"—it means to widen one's periphery to take in more of the world. If a stimulus is introduced to an unprepared person, his eyes narrow and the flight/fight response takes over. If the same unexpected stimulus comes to someone with "soft eyes," the natural reflex is transcended and a more authentic response takes its place—such as thinking a new thought.
>
> Soft eyes, it seems to me, is an evocative image for what happens when we gaze on sacred reality. Now our eyes are open and receptive, able to take in the greatness of the world and the grace of great things.[10]

Taking in "the grace of great things" may well be an alternate definition of gratitude. Seeing with "soft eyes" alerts us to gratefulness in our present lives.

Sometimes gratitude hides at the edges of our experience. Like when I was fired. Although I eventually learned gratitude through hindsight, I was also nurturing a capacity for soft eyes at the time—and that was helping me see gratitude even then. Although it was initially difficult to apprehend, many good things happened as that position ended. I had begun writing for the local newspaper, the university across town invited me to teach part-time, and I made many new friends. People went out of their way to be kind to me, opened new professional doors, and listened when I was near despair. Despite losing a job, I had just enough money to get by. I joined a wonderful new church, and I met the man who would become my life partner. I stopped focusing on immediate worries—and learned to look toward the edges of life's surprises.

The gratitude journal reminded me to look toward the periphery of blessings. I had to look beyond challenges to find the larger "grace of great things" that sometimes seems to hide just out of view. I was learning a new perspective, orienting my life toward new horizons, and discovering that gratitude could guide me as I moved ahead. The widely quoted wisdom of poet Maya Angelou became real: "If you must look back, do so forgivingly. If you must look forward, do so prayerfully. However, the wisest thing you can do is be present in the present . . . gratefully." Seeing with soft eyes opens a wider vision of present circumstances, lessens fear and anxiety, and alerts us to new possibilities for our lives.

Future, or Foresight: When we reflect on gratitude and time, it is not hard to see how we can be thankful for what has happened in the past and what is occurring in our lives now. But the future? How does gratitude relate to that?

David DeSteno, a professor at Northeastern University, makes this case:

> When life's got you down, gratitude can seem like a chore. Sure, you'll go through the motions and say the right things. . . . But you might not truly feel grateful in your heart. It can be like saying "I'm happy for you" to someone who just got the job you wanted. The words and the feelings often don't match.
>
> This disconnect is unfortunate, though. It comes

from a somewhat misguided view that gratitude is all about looking backward—back to what has already been. But in reality, that's not how gratitude truly works. At a psychological level, gratitude isn't about passive reflection; it's about building resilience. It's not about being thankful for things that have already occurred and, thus, can't be changed; it's about ensuring the benefits of what comes next. It's about making sure that tomorrow, and the day after, you will have something to be grateful for.[11]

When psychologists speak of resilience, they are referring to our capacity to grow into our best selves—to be healthy, creative, emotionally balanced, and mature people. Positive emotions, like gratitude, foster resiliency, which strengthens our physical health, especially our heart health and the ability to recover more quickly from illness and surgery. Thus, gratitude can actually create better outcomes in our future health. Resiliency also works to improve psychological health. According to one study, "resilient individuals reported fewer symptoms of depression and trauma" following the September 11, 2001, terrorist attacks.[12] Having a grateful disposition in advance of that national crisis gave some Americans better coping skills and helped them navigate those frightening and difficult days with fewer negative effects than their fellow citizens. Researchers discovered that positive emotions "not only make people feel good in the present, but they also increase the likelihood that people will function well and feel good in the future" and cause an "upward spiral" of well-being.[13] Gratitude now anticipates increased positive emotions in the future.

But gratitude now and in the future also arises from practice.

When I had lost my job and I did not generally *feel* grateful, I joined a new church. At a moment of deep despair and isolation, I heard that a minister at Trinity Episcopal Church in Santa Barbara—a church I did not attend—had mounted a campaign among mainline Protestant clergy in town to try to pressure the college to keep me on. Their effort failed. But I could not believe that a pastor whom I had never met would see the injustice of my situation and try to do something about it.

I still remember how completely surprised and utterly humbled I felt upon learning about his effort. I made an appointment to meet him to thank him for what he had done. We became friends. As a result of his action and the gratitude I experienced in response, I joined the church he served. Although we were not really thinking about it, we had enacted gratitude—he did something for my benefit, and I responded by both saying thank you and becoming a member of the congregation. We bonded through gift and gratitude.

That bond, with its resulting participation in Trinity Church, in turn created more bonds. The people in that community were some of the most giving human beings I have ever known, and the church existed as a continually expanding circle of gifts and appreciation in which individuals were sometimes benefactors and oftentimes beneficiaries. We were all givers and receivers. I had no way of knowing in advance, but the friendships forged around the practice of gratitude at Trinity formed the basis of my future life—everything from becoming a writer to getting married again and having a child.

Life in that church consisted of mutual support and mutual gifts, and because of that mutuality we developed healthy obligations to one another and deepened our capacity to trust. This was not a quid pro quo exchange in which we earned credit from one another for good works; it was instead a dynamic structure of relationships that ensured the existence of a community of care stretching into the future. More than a positive emotion, this sort of gratitude became the foundation of my healing and deepened my ability to take risks and make good choices for the next decade of my life. It went well beyond the immediate event of saying thank you.

PRACTICE TAKES TIME. A well-known rule of practice says that to become an expert at something, you need to devote ten thousand hours to doing it. Gratitude is not a practice that can be counted in hours. Instead, it invites us to engage the longer arc of time. In order for it to become a habit, it asks that we attend to seeing time more fully: engaging the past more graciously, living more appreciatively now, and building thanks into the foundation of our future. Attending to our lives with hindsight, wide sight, and foresight moves gratefulness from emotion to ethic. Thus, gratitude may feel good—and those good feelings do good things for us—but as an ethical disposition, gratitude is a strong basis for creating a good life. The habit of gratefulness helps us thrive. It not only takes time, but it can change the way we experience the times of our lives.

4

Intentional Practice

Like other forms of practice, gratefulness makes
us more resilient and flexible, and also offers
a way to frame and learn from everything
that unfolds in our lives.

—KRISTI NELSON

On September 22, 2015, Phyllis Tickle, one of the wisest spiritual writers in recent decades, died at age eighty-one. Phyllis was many things—a devotional writer, a poet, a playwright, a journalist, and a professor. And, indeed, she was a friend. She did not die quickly. Diagnosed with cancer at the beginning of 2015, she spent those last months writing colleagues. My e-mail is full of exchanges from that time. At first our notes were gossipy and hopeful, but they turned more serious as the weeks unfolded. Toward the end, they consisted mostly of my sending her poetry and short letters of gratitude and her returning increasingly brief replies. About five weeks before she passed away, her final substantial note to me read:

> Thanks, dear heart, for the prayers. Things wind down here, slowly but surely, and I am mightily content that it should be so. It is good to have this time between the knowing and the actual ending. Obviously we all "know" it, but to have so specific and well-defined a time frame is a benison, and I am grateful.

She faced death as she had learned to live life—thankfully.

"What remarkable calm," I thought as I read her note. I also knew I would not sound quite so thankful. I suspected that I would be raging against death. Having lived eight decades, however, Phyllis understood gratitude in the story of past, present, and future. I have rarely known anyone who said thank you and meant it as deeply as she. The equanimity with which Phyllis embraced her earthly end was shaped by lifelong habits of gratefulness. Of all her practices of gratitude, the most important was her commitment to praying four times each day a set of traditional Christian prayers of praise and thanksgiving. Phyllis knew that the long story of our lives is made up of precious hours and days, and paying attention to the daily cycle of time is keenly important in shaping a life of gratitude. She wrote a series of books on the subject, a set of prayer guides thick with praise and thanksgivings.

Our days are so steeped in routine and habits that most are invisible to us. However, we tend to organize and attend to daily time in patterns generally related to work. Most people wake up with the sun, go to work in fields, homes, or offices, break at midday, finish work, and end the day with a meal and rest. This everyday round is sometimes marked by religious observance, punctuated by prayers, bells, and calls to devotion. For more than a thousand years in Christian societies, the hours of work were interwoven with hours of prayer, forming a cycle of morning, noon, and evening rituals practiced by laity, monks, nuns, and priests. The same is true for Muslims, Jews, and Buddhists. The hallowing of the hours in a day is fundamental to a faithful life, and remembering blessings and giving thanks is a shared practice across world religions.

Phyllis knew the connection between work and thanks. On more than one occasion, I watched her leave a meeting or conference room to go and pray. She would step out briefly, open a book, utter a few ancient words, and come back into the group—often picking up exactly where she had left off. As a mentor, she taught many things. None, however, struck so close to the heart as her natural habit of giving thanks in prayer.

MINDING THE DAY

The practice of hourly thanksgiving has faded in modern society, where secularism and pluralism generally inhibit public rituals of thanksgiving. You still see it in places like Assisi or Mecca or Katmandu, where bells and minarets and gongs still call the populace to prayer. But, for the most part, public prayers have given way to private ones, often in simplified forms. In some Christian churches, such a practice is known as "daily devotions." I grew up Methodist—and despite the fact that John

Wesley, the founder of Methodism, was famous for his regular practice of daily prayer—such piety was largely lost to us.

I first encountered daily devotions long before my friendship with Phyllis. Instead, I discovered the practice of daily prayer when I was a teenager at an evangelical church. I will never forget my friend Phil, who woke up before dawn and spent an hour in prayer. His Bible was worn from use, and I suspect his knees were too. At sixteen, he seemed holy.

The entire business of daily devotions flummoxed me, though. I asked Phil what he did for an hour. He replied that he read the Bible, took notes, marked the bits of scripture that spoke to him, memorized verses, offered thanks for the day, and then prayed for his needs and the needs of others. I made a valiant effort to imitate his piety. But I failed. I did, however, mess up several Bibles with yellow highlighters. But I never could understand prayer. The whole business seemed like some sort of magic trick—praying for God to pay attention to a crisis and fix it? Intercessory prayer of this nature made me wonder if God was not a divine vending machine. Put in the right change and get out what you wanted. A spiritual quid pro quo? The exercise puzzled me.

As a result, I began collecting prayer books. If I could not pray well on my own, I figured I could learn. When I first started reading prayer books, I noticed that most had personal supplications that were topically arranged: for illness, healing, children, grief, job loss, financial struggle, and so on. Other books ranged more widely, with prayers for justice, peace, world mission, and poverty. When I joined an Episcopal church, I discovered a small section (a mere seven pages long) in the Book of Common Prayer called "Daily Devotions for Individuals and Families." Of all the pages in that complicated prayer book, they came to mean the most to me. Those brief pages were the remnant of the ancient Christian tradition of praying the Liturgy of the Hours (also called the Divine Office or Daily Office) at morning, noon, early evening, and night.

For most of my early twenties, praying through those short liturgies became a lifeline. I especially loved the morning words: "Open my lips, O Lord, and my mouth shall proclaim your praise!" The brief bits of scripture interspersed with traditional Anglican written prayers framed my days. What I appreciated most were its brief readings—texts not dependent on me for complex study. The days could be marked not by heroic spiritual exertion, but by simple, moving phrases of blessing, scripture, prayer, and assurance. And always thanks.

Those devotions alerted me to the ancient practice of the Hours. About a decade later, Phyllis and I became friends. One of her great projects was a three-volume prayer manual for the Daily Office, and those devotionals now sit on my shelf. Next to her books is a wide array of contemporary versions of the Hours and daily prayer, evidence that the practice has been undergoing a renaissance in the last two decades. I do not pray any of them as I should, but I have learned something quite simple from all of them. The ancient practice did not involve an hour-long Bible study with a highlighter—nor did it focus on getting something from God. Almost every rite of prayer at every hour of the day in each of those books begins in a similar way, with a form of thanks:

> O come, let us sing to the LORD;
> let us make a joyful noise to the rock of our
> salvation!

Let us come into his presence with thanksgiving;
let us make a joyful noise to him with songs of
praise!

PSALM 95:1–2

The daily Hours do not focus on what we want or need. The Hours start with gratitude. Ancient Christian wisdom is that the first words of each day should be those of thanks.

Of course, Christian prayers direct praise and gratefulness to God, who is understood to be the giver of all gifts. The same is true for Jewish prayers. My friend David Gregory, journalist and author, who is quite serious in his Jewish faith, opens his day with these words: "I offer thanks to You, living and eternal King, for You have mercifully restored my soul within me; Your faithfulness is great."[1] Muslims and other theists have similar practices. But one need not believe in God to give thanks. It is just as possible to begin a day by directing thanks toward the rhythm of nature whereby the sun rises or the body awakens, to farmers who grew the food for our breakfast, or to workers in a foreign land who made the clothes we put on our backs. "Open my lips! May thanks come forth!" The point is to start each day remembering that life is a gift and that we are interdependent with sacred presence, natural forces, and human relationships even as we wake. In a very real way, morning gratitude is a primary form of mindfulness, a practice of paying attention to abundance and life.

In order to "mind the day," I keep a single page of gratitude prayers by my bed, and I read one each morning. This is a recent page, with gratefulness meditations from a naturalist, a Buddhist monk, a poet, and two Christian writers:

Awakening
in a moment of peace
I give thanks
to the source of all peace

as I set forth
into the day
the birds sing
with new voices
and I listen
with new ears
and give thanks[2]

HARRIET KOFALK

Waking up this morning, I see the blue sky
I join my hands in thanks for the many wonders of life;
for having twenty-four brand new hours.
The sun is rising on the forest
and so is my awareness.[3]

THICH NHAT HANH

i thank You God for most this amazing
day: for the leaping greenly spirits of trees
and a blue true dream of sky; and for everything
which is natural which is infinite which is yes[4]

E. E. CUMMINGS

For the freshness of this new day
thanks be to you, O God.
For morning's gift of clarity

its light like the first day's dawn
thanks be to you.
In this newborn light
let us see afresh.
In this gateway onto what has never been before
let our soul breathe hope
for the earth
for the creatures
for the human family.
Let our soul breathe hope.[5]

JOHN PHILIP NEWELL

With the morning birdsong,
My heart echoes thank you.
With the rustling sounds in the kitchen,
My heart echoes thank you.
With the early noise of the suburbs,
My heart echoes thank you.
With the awakening words of day,
I add my voice and say thank you.

I wrote the last one. My family laughs about it, because I frequently complain of being shaken from sleep by either a noisy lawn service or my neighbor's motorcycle. But, as I pointed out, that was what I most needed—to be able to say thank you first thing in the morning, a leaf blower or obnoxious machine notwithstanding. Gratitude sets the intention for the day, reminding us to notice blessings and gifts as we move through the hours ahead.

I have come to think of hourly prayer as punctuating time with gratitude. Meals, especially lunch and dinner, are good times to say thank you. Noon provides a check on the day, a moment to reaffirm an intention toward gratefulness. In my family, even at the hardest spiritual times, we have always said grace at dinner. This old-fashioned practice, of saying thank you over our evening meal, has grounded us for two decades.[6] Believe me, it is not always lyrical or deep. But it is a moment to remind us that we are receivers of the gifts of food and health, to appreciate joys and successes, and to be open for what we—and others—need. Apparently, we are not alone in this practice. According to a recent poll, nearly half of all Americans say grace before meals at least a few times a week, either as a ritual prayer or a spontaneous one.[7]

If morning marks the intention to live the day gratefully, night is the time to review, reflect, and offer thanksgiving. Many spiritual guides recommend writing a few things you were grateful for in a journal shortly before going to sleep, times during the day when you felt moments of abundance and joy. The Jesuits, the Roman Catholic monastic order of which Pope Francis is a member, recommend a prayerful evening review of the day, a practice they call the *examen* (Latin, "examination"). It involves five simple steps and centers on gratefulness:

1. Become aware of God's presence.
2. Review the day with gratitude.
3. Pay attention to your emotions.
4. Choose one feature of the day and pray from it.
5. Look toward tomorrow.

This need not be a long or involved process. Instead, its simple format serves to mark the day's end in a way that draws the mind and heart toward grace and gifts. Notice that the *examen* asks you to review with gratitude and then consider your emotions. This is not a random reflection on your feelings; instead, it focuses on emotions after you recall blessings. There is a spiritual flow in these steps: awareness, gratitude, affirmations, prayer, and hope. The *examen* intentionally orders thoughts, closing the day with thanksgiving and setting positive expectations for tomorrow.

Of course, one need not be a Jesuit—or even a Christian—to find the five steps of the *examen* meaningful. They are one way to recount gratitude in a day. Writing in a journal, remembering the good things of the day, making a list of the people who were kind or helpful to you, counting beads of blessing on a bracelet or rosary, and thinking about pleasant experiences offer the same opportunity for thankfulness. On Twitter, Parker Molloy, a widely followed journalist and LGBTQ activist, maintains a nightly "thankfulness thread," to which she posts one daily thing for which she is grateful, ranging from her dog or the weather to sharing a good dinner with her partner. It is the last thing she does on social media to end the day. You can sense how, after the rough-and-tumble of controversial political comment, giving thanks grounds her spirituality.

Not only is this a beneficial spiritual practice; several scientific studies have shown that people who practice gratitude right before bedtime sleep better, more soundly, and more deeply. An evening ritual of thanksgiving allows you to end the day with less stress and a greater capacity to rest. The Buddha offered these words to sum up the day:

> Let us rise up and be thankful,
> for if we didn't learn a lot today,
> at least we learned a little,

and if we didn't learn a little,
at least we didn't get sick,
and if we got sick,
at least we didn't die;
so, let us all be thankful.[8]

Or as one psychologist suggests for reviewing the day: "Count blessings, not sheep."[9]

More than forty years ago, when I asked my friend Phil about his morning devotions, I never imagined that it was the first step to discovering that the hours of each day can be marked with gratitude. Not only should we give thanks in all things; we can give thanks at all times. With practice and with ever widening awareness, we see that gratitude frames our days. This day. This hour. Right now.

BLESSINGS

Years ago, I had a friend—I will call her Elizabeth—who was kind, generous, smart, and appreciated by others for her open-handedness. I liked her for these qualities. She was, however, at the same time a surprisingly negative person.

Elizabeth had grown up in a wealthy family who lived in a posh suburb, attended a private school, and had traveled the world widely. She was cultured and seemed to have everything—beautiful clothes, expensive furniture, new cars, a first-rate education. In the future, she stood to inherit a fortune. I was in awe of her. She possessed every advantage in life, having things I could barely dream existed. It amazed me that she would even want to be my friend.

I mentioned my admiration—if not my envy—to a mutual acquaintance. She replied, "Perhaps you shouldn't feel that way. You know, Elizabeth's had a really hard life."

"What?" I responded.

"She's had to fight for so many things," she continued, and then she listed a long litany of difficulties Elizabeth had experienced.

That conversation made me notice what had escaped my notice before: my friend—who had so much—often spoke of what she did not have and the burdens she carried. No one's life is perfect, of course, but she portrayed herself as uniquely challenged, plagued by misunderstandings and hardship. She rarely spoke of her multitude of gifts as blessings. Instead, she minimized good things and went out of her way to not mention them. Whenever I spoke of some financial or personal struggle I was having, she replied by reciting the obstacles she had faced. After a while, it felt like a competition to see who had the worst life circumstances to overcome.

Although our friendship lasted for years, it was never very stable. I always wanted to shout, "Please! Just appreciate the many advantages you have in life!" But I never did. The whole thing dissolved into mutual resentment. There was no talk of blessings. Our friendship broke apart in that competition for "life's toughest path." Instead of "one-upping" each other with blessings, we "one-downed" each other with failures. In the end, we could not even be grateful for one another.

One of the most interesting studies related to gratitude explores the difficulties and advantages in our lives as "headwinds" and "tailwinds." Headwinds are the resistance one encounters in a race, when "the wind is literally in one's face." Tailwinds are the opposite, the "wind at one's back." Researchers Shai Davidai and Thomas Gilovich discovered that people tend to pay more attention to life's headwinds, because they are harder to overcome.[10] We ignore tailwinds because we adjust to the advantages they give us. Tailwind benefits tend to be invisible. But headwinds? We boast of fighting them.

We remember difficult challenges more vividly than what comes easily to us. Because we pay more attention to what is hard, what we feel we have worked for, we tend to believe that our own life has been full of "barriers and challenges . . . more severe than those experienced by others." This belief, in turn, causes envy. How? As the researchers note, "When people (falsely) believe that their road has been especially difficult, they can easily become resentful of those they (falsely) believe have had an easier path," resulting in feelings of thwarted entitlement. "The flip side of this toxic stew of resentment, envy, and entitlement," claim Davidai and Gilovich, "is gratitude." When we overvalue the struggle and challenge of headwinds, we miss the opportunity to be grateful for the gifts, the tailwinds, that assist us. "An understanding of how easy it is for people to get in touch with their headwinds," suggest the authors, "and how hard it is to fully appreciate their tailwinds can help explain why a consistent connection to gratitude can be so elusive."[11]

Sometimes, we might speak of nice things as "blessings," a kind of pious way of talking about material comfort or personal privilege. But what if "blessings" are, at least in part, the "tailwinds" of our lives? The invisible benefits that are conferred on us—everything from political policies to economic advantages to social relationships—and that we receive unnoticed are, indeed, blessings. In this framework, blessings emerge as the contributions others have made to our lives, either as personal gifts or gifts of a larger community (things such as a good public school paid for by tax money). Blessings are not pious rewards for good behavior. Blessings are the "boost" bestowed on us by systems, structures, families, and other benefactors who assist us on our way.

Headwinds: barriers. Tailwinds: blessings. Headwinds make us say, "I earned this." Tailwinds should not be invisible. Instead, they should call forth, "I received this. I am so grateful."[12]

This helps explain what happened with Elizabeth. Her headwinds of difficulty were invisible to me, but her tailwinds of privilege were not. It was just the opposite for her. The burdens she found painful she magnified, but the "boosts" of wealth she paid no attention to. To be honest, my headwinds always had to do with money, and my tailwinds (things I generally ignored) were things she admired.

When the friendship ended, I reflected on what had happened. Instead of focusing on her failure to see her blessings (and my resulting envy of her blessings), I began to consider my own blessings (those things she might have seen that eluded me), like intellectual curiosity and social ease. Schoolwork and friendships were my tailwinds. I loved to read, learn, and write. I was an extrovert and loved people and parties. But I rarely paid attention to these things. They were simply the gifts of my life. However, I always worried about paying tuition, supporting myself, and having a functioning car. I remember the difficulty of working four jobs in graduate school just to stay afloat and trying to survive after losing that first job. There were headwinds aplenty.

As a result of failing at my friendship with Elizabeth, however, I took stock. I assessed my own life more realistically. I realized that getting good grades and being well liked were not irrelevant to the person I had become. They were blessings—boosts given to me through DNA, growing up in a decent suburb in postwar America, having caring teachers and mentors, and my mother's endless cheerleading. The headwinds can still command my attention, but tailwinds are more obvious to me now than ever. I continue to understand the privileges that have boosted me, appreciate what was good about them, and work to make sure others experience more tailwinds than headwinds.[13] The tailwinds are gifts, and being aware of them makes me more grateful and, I hope, generous.

CHOOSING GRATITUDE AS A WAY OF LIFE

A friend of mine recently went through a painful personal crisis. At first, it seemed to be the result of a breakup. Then it went deeper, as he realized that he did not understand the meaning or purpose of his own life. He was both anxious and depressed. "I think," he confessed, "that I'm really having a spiritual crisis."

After many long talks about faith, I finally gave him a small book of gratitude quotes. I suggested that he might take his focus off feelings of loss and, instead, try to find something good each day. I hoped he might see how much there was to be thankful for—that despite immediate challenges he was a gifted person with much to offer the world. Maybe looking for gratitude could help him find his way.

A couple days later, he texted me a quote from the book that had spoken to him: "God, help me to quiet my noisy, worrisome mind in my ordinary world. Help me to relax in the familiar and to be aware of and appreciate it."

Of all the possible quotes in the book for him to choose, this one surprised me. I had expected something more straightforward, perhaps comforting words about gifts and abundance. But his quote was a prayer: "God, help me." With what? "To relax in the familiar and to be aware of and appreciate it." My friend was not asking for a dramatic healing, for answers to be written in the sky, or for God to fix his problems. He wanted to see the world around him more fully and deeply, to develop greater awareness, and to be grateful for what was already there.

When I read his text, I thought, "Well, isn't that what we all need to do?"

That is what a practice of gratitude comes to. All around us, every day, there are gifts. Whether we are facing a crisis or not, no matter our challenges or feelings, there are gifts, most of which go unnoticed, unappreciated, and often disregarded. Sometimes they take us by surprise—we experience the "aha" of being helped or suddenly seeing a beautiful sunset, and the emotion of gratitude wells up in our being. Gifts seem to spring upon us like an epiphany, bursting our hearts with that wild admixture of humility and joy that we know as gratitude.

But if we cultivate our awareness to see those gifts more often, with clearer and more consistent vision, something else happens. Thankfulness becomes more habitual, a regular part of how we respond to the world. Yes, gratitude still holds the power to surprise and to elicit a strong emotional response. However, as a habit, it also becomes a steadying companion, incorporated into the story of our lives. Gratitude is not just a knock-your-socks-off revelation of goodness and beauty; it emerges as a daily—even hourly—disposition of appreciation toward familiar gifts, including the tailwinds of blessing.

This kind of paying attention is often referred to as mindfulness. I like that word, and that more people are embracing practices of mindfulness. But I think mindfulness involves choosing too. We can choose to believe that we are autonomous beings in complete command of our own lives, reliant upon no one and nothing but ourselves. We can choose to focus on our failures or our losses, on what we feel entitled to or what we deserve. We can choose anger, fear, resentment, grief, hubris, or pain. We can choose to live our lives stuck in our worst moments. We can choose to believe that everyone and everything are against us. We can choose to define ourselves on the basis of someone else's violence, prejudice, or injustice toward us. We can choose to define life as a zero-sum game. We can choose every negative philosophy, theology, or ideology that cuts us off from grace, and we can choose to think there is no one and nothing to thank.

Even if we make good choices, it can be hard to follow through: the failed diet, the broken New Year's resolution, the long-distance friendship that gets neglected, the gratitude practice that falls by the wayside. It often seems that the more steel will we apply to a desire to change, the more miserable the failure. We all know this—even those we consider saints knew it as well. In the New Testament book of Romans, St. Paul cries out in frustration: "I do not understand my own actions. For I do not do what I want, but I do the very thing I hate!" (7:15).

In that passage, Paul is making a rather complicated—and distinctively Christian—argument about human behavior and sin. But Paul solves his dilemma in a way that goes beyond a Christian response and is widely applicable to practicing gratitude in any tradition. "For those who live according to the flesh set their minds on the flesh," he proclaims, "but those who live according to the Spirit set their minds on things of the Spirit" (Rom. 8:5). Or, as Jesus put it, "Where your treasure is, there your heart will be also" (Matt. 6:21). Both Paul and Jesus are speaking of our inclinations. Do our desires incline toward what we think we have earned or deserve (the "flesh"), or are they drawn toward a life of appreciation and grace (the "spirit")? Where is your treasure? Your heart? Which direction do you choose? What draws your soul?

If you choose ingratitude, I cannot help you. But most of us do not willingly say, "I have decided to live my life free from thanksgiving." Even at ungrateful moments, we feel the tug toward something else. But it can be hard to get there. Ingratitude often results from misunderstanding the nature of thanks, failing to see the larger picture of our lives, or forgetting to nurture a spirit of gratefulness. We ignore the tailwinds. Instead, we fixate on what has hindered us, and that mutates into envy and entitlement. When we neglect gratitude, we are, in effect, making a choice toward negative emotions, which in turn foster more negativity.

But when, if even for a little while, we choose gratefulness, that choice builds on itself and begins to create a spiral of appreciation. The first choice—even if only a vague inclination—sets up the next choice, and the next, and the next one beyond that. Thus, when we "do the very thing we hate," it is often because we have helped to create an environment of "the flesh" in our own lives. We have made a habit of things we do not want to do; they are reflexive. We do not intentionally choose ingratitude. We choose it because we have made a habit of it, and we are not even always aware of the negative habit we have constructed. "The real power of habit," claims Charles Duhigg, is "the insight that your habits are what you choose them to be."[14]

To choose gratitude is not an act of dogged determination. To choose gratitude is to hear an inner urging toward thanks, to be aware of the grace in life, and to respond. This urging comes from what Paul calls "spirit" and Jesus calls "heart." And, for whatever reason, we turn. That single turn is a choice; it is not as much will as it is a reply to an invitation for a deeper, better life.

We may start gratitude practices like writing a journal or listing daily blessings, succeed for a time, and then forget and fail. But—and this is the important part—even if a specific technique fails, it has helped to create a larger environment of gratefulness. Interventions may be short term, techniques difficult to maintain, practices hard to master. But these actions will have shaped a spiritual habitat in which new habits can form. In that environment, it becomes easier to choose gratitude the next time, with fewer struggles and less guilt, and eventually thanksgiving becomes habitual. Thus, habits seed a spiritual habitat in which we can dwell in greater awareness of gratitude, so that gratitude enters in and inhabits us. We can intentionally practice gratitude—through greater awareness, through specific techniques, by developing new routines, and by strengthening habits of gratitude. As we do these things, gratefulness becomes part of who we are.

English essayist Samuel Johnson once said, "Gratitude is a fruit of great cultivation." The Christian scriptures liken gratitude to joy, a "fruit of the spirit." Gratitude is not only an emotion; it is something we do. But it is not a program. It is like tending a garden. It takes planting and watering and weeding. It takes time and attention. It takes learning. It takes routine. But, eventually, the ground yields, shoots come forth, and thanksgiving blooms.

III

We: Emotions
Joy and Celebration

Praise song for struggle, praise song for the day.
Praise song for every hand-lettered sign,
the figuring-it-out at kitchen tables.
Some live by *love thy neighbor as thyself*,
others by *first do no harm* or *take no more
than you need*. What if the mightiest word is love?

—ELIZABETH ALEXANDER

5

Grateful Together

Gratitude is happiness doubled by wonder.

—G. K. CHESTERTON

We arrived fairly early, but it was already uncomfortably hot, and there was stiff competition for parking places. We faced a long walk to the venue and the possibility of getting stuck in the nosebleed seats. We wanted to beat the crowds, but when we pulled into the parking lot, we knew we had failed. Dozens and dozens of ebullient teenagers carrying identical blue academic regalia were headed toward the arena. Trailing behind them were parents, siblings, grandparents, and friends holding congratulatory signs, blue and white balloons, and bouquets of roses.

My daughter shook with anxiety and excitement. After four years of hard work, she had finished with honors and was headed to college in the fall. This was an end, and this was a new beginning. As we got out of the car, she glanced at the legions of her classmates and then turned a nervous smile in my direction. I patted her on the back and gave her a little hug. We gathered up her robe and stole. We joined the advancing throng, all there to celebrate high school graduation.

The day ahead would be long with speeches, awards, and six hundred students called forward to receive diplomas. Our local high school, West Potomac High School, is a huge public school with a diverse student body. Forty percent of the students are white, 30 percent Hispanic, 20 percent black, and the rest Asian, Native American, and biracial. Even though it is part of the well-regarded Fairfax County school system in Virginia, West Potomac's student body is not particularly wealthy. Government statistics say that 38 percent of the students are "economically disadvantaged," and a large number are either immigrants or first-generation Americans. Just like our neighborhood.

We found some seats not unreasonably far from the action, and I searched the stands for familiar faces. I did not immediately see anyone I knew. We had never been at a school-wide event before (most of the things we attended at her school involved the honor students and the crew team), and I could not help but notice the incredible diversity of the crowd. I had not been to a high school graduation since my own, more than thirty years ago, from Saguaro High School, in Scottsdale, Arizona. Scottsdale was—and still is—a very white and very rich place. I think my high school class included one biracial family, a few recent immigrants from Middle Eastern countries, and a dozen or so Hispanics. At Saguaro, we pretty much all looked like cousins, spoke the same language, and shared similar customs and manners.

As we waited for my daughter's class to enter the arena, I did not even recognize the languages being spoken around us, nor could I place much of the native dress worn by mothers, aunts, and grandmothers. Our little nuclear family group seemed so contained, so introverted, and so northern European, surrounded as we were by huge clans of people from Latin America and Africa. When the band struck up the entrance march and the students began filing in, huge roars went up from the crowd. This was more like World Cup soccer (although the school board specifically had banned vuvuzelas) than any high school graduation in my experience. When they called out the graduates by name, nearly everyone ignored the directive to hold their applause. Instead, families hooted and whistled, waved banners, and made a ruckus of praise for their son or daughter. I knew the exercises would be long, but I never guessed they would be so loud.

At first I felt uncomfortable. My husband, perhaps sensing this, said, "Notice—almost every group that cheers is an immigrant family. I bet their children are the first to graduate from an American school!" He went on, "For some of these folks, the students might be the very first to ever go so far in school. That's the whole reason they came here. They're noisy because they are so grateful."

Although we certainly could not survey every family from where we were sitting, it appeared he was right. We were not just at a graduation. We were sitting in an arena of thanksgiving, where hundreds of people were feeling grateful together. Some were thankful a son or daughter did well and anticipated the new adventure of college ahead. For them, graduation was a growing-up marker, a pause on the road toward the next thing, and they were offering appropriate thanks for a job well done. Others, however, seemed wildly grateful for this single moment as an all-out celebration for a goal achieved, the fruit of family sacrifice, the reward of a new life in a place of safety and success, the fulfillment of a dream.

As I watched all these new Americans rejoice, my soul moved from discomfort to appreciation. I felt thankful for the school district and teachers who made this miracle happen, for this good use of our taxes, and for the neighborhood that is home for all of us. As more and more graduates came forward, the crowd got louder and louder. Eventually, a kind of uninhibited thankfulness swept everyone—including our small family—into its chorus. When the last name was called, the graduates threw their caps in the air and released primal whoops of joy. Families jumped from their seats, shouting bravo and pumping fists into the air. People poured out of the exits, hugging one another, laughing and crying and taking pictures. Amid the thousands, a spontaneous litany emerged: "What a great day!" "We're so proud of you!" "Thank you, Jesus!" "Mom and dad, thanks so much!"

It was hard to find our daughter amid the grateful mob. But as I searched, I enjoyed winding through the crowd of my neighbors—from all social classes, from many races and nations—and eavesdropping on their thankfulness. I thought back to Saguaro, where a single clergyperson gave a benediction—a prayer of blessing—as our graduation ended. We had waited for someone to lead us in gratitude. Here, there had been no religious professional to offer up our thanksgiving. Instead, we had done it ourselves. It was not particularly reverent, but it was fun.

GRATITUDE IS SOCIAL

Strange thing about gratitude—it always comes with a preposition. We are grateful *for* something, grateful *to* someone, and, often, grateful *with* others. Even in untargeted gratitude and when you are completely alone, prepositions show up. Imagine you need to get away, perhaps to struggle with a decision or a grief. During the winter, a friend loans you her beach house. It is the off-season, and you are alone. One morning, you wake up and walk at the water's edge. The sun is rising, colors shimmer off the waves, painting them shades of blue, pink, and silver unlike any you have ever seen.

All of a sudden, your heart opens up. You feel grateful *for* the beautiful sunrise, grateful *to* your friend, and grateful *with* the soaring seabirds. There are no other human beings, but you experience gratitude. And, surprisingly enough, you also make community. In that moment, no matter how isolated the shore, gratitude connects you to nature's rhythms, to a distant friend, and to other creatures. The sun and sea offer their gifts— indiscriminately, as they always do—but you still say "thanks" to them, to your friend, perhaps to God. There, on a deserted beach, gifts are given and received, praise returned, and a new awareness of connection comes alive. When it comes to gratitude, "me" always leads to "we." "Gratitude takes us outside ourselves," insists Robert Emmons, "where we see ourselves as part of a larger, intricate network of sustaining relationships, relationships that are mutually reciprocal."[1]

On November 22, 2015, Pastor Jason Micheli stood in the pulpit at Aldersgate United Methodist Church in Alexandria, Virginia, and preached a sermon on gratitude. It was right before Thanksgiving, and it was the church's stewardship season, a time when congregations are urged to consider gifts and generosity. In the autumn, a gratitude sermon was nothing out of the ordinary.

But this was not an ordinary day. Jason, a forty-something father with young children, was preaching for the first time in nearly a year—since being diagnosed with and treated for a rare and incurable form of cancer. He was better, and the cancer was "controlled," but, as the congregation knew, he would have to do chemo every two months for the rest of his life. He stood in the pulpit, barely out of treatment, to preach a thanksgiving sermon for his community.

He began: "You all have done so much for us. You've fed us and prayed for us and with us. You've helped us with my medical bills, and you've sat with me in the hospital. You were there to catch me when I passed out in the chemo room, and you didn't bat an eye when I puked in your car."

But, he said, as much as he appreciated it, he actually hated all that help. "I've always been awful at receiving gifts," he admitted, "I hate feeling like I'm in another's debt. . . . I was a guy who kept score, which means I didn't mind you being in my debt. I just didn't want to be in yours."

But he learned something: Gratitude is not about repayment of debts. It is about relationships. Through his cancer, Jason discovered that courage and hope could not be summoned magically; rather, strength and healing came through community. He spoke of the church's greatest gift to his family in crisis: "We can endure all things because you've been with us. You're *with* us. More so than all the stuff you've done *for* us, you've been *with* us."

With no dry eye in the congregation, he continued, "It was kind of you to share my nightmare. It was kind of you to share in my pain and suffering. It was kind of you to share in Ali's worry, in my boys' fears and anxiety. It was kind of you to make my cancer—our cancer—yours too."

"Thank you," he finished, "for being with me."[2]

Gratitude is social. It is about, as Pastor Jason learned, "presence, participation, and partnership." It is about being *with* one another, *in* life together. It is the thread of nature and neighbor, the seemingly fragile strands of gifts and goodness that weave our lives together.

BREAKING DOWN WALLS

A few months after a white supremacist walked into Emanuel AME Church in Charleston, South Carolina, and killed nine people, I stood outside the building at the makeshift memorial to the victims. As I stared at the flowers and letters marking this sad and sacred place, contemplating the legacy of slavery and the evil of racism, I caught sight of two African American men at the periphery. With flowers in hand, they were waiting to approach the wall. I stepped aside to make way for them.

After a few minutes of quiet reflection, the men attempted to take a selfie in front of the church. They were not very good at it.

"Would you like me to take your picture?" I asked.

"Yes, please," one responded as he handed me his cell phone. I snapped their picture, making sure that the photos had turned out well. I had done so with a reverence I hoped was appropriate to the moment. I held out the phone to return it to its owner, but not before he said, "We came a long way to be here. Thank you so much."

I replied, "I'm so sorry. It is the least I can do. It was awful . . . just . . . I'm so sorry . . ." My voice broke a little.

Instead of reaching for the phone, the man reached toward me and gave me a hug, one of those side-by-side hugs sometimes offered by strangers. Together we stood at the wall in a companionable silence that seemed to mix grief and gratitude. For a moment, another sort of wall—the wall of human division—at least cracked and let grace through. He turned, as did his friend, they both shook my hand, and we parted ways. I felt grateful to have been there, grateful for their presence. The hugs and their willingness to share their silence seemed like a gift.

Although we feel grateful as individuals and can develop spiritual and ethical practices of gratitude in our personal lives, the deepest experiences of gratitude move us beyond islands of isolation into connection and community. Feeling grateful causes us to reach out toward its perceived source. "Gratitude only happens when we get a real gift," one ethicist says, and "a real gift comes with a giver attached."[3] In the case of the sunrise, it might mean lifting our hands in praise to the sky or to God. In the case of another person, it typically means expressing thanks through a hug. Indeed, "hugging is perceived as one of the most central and positive features of gratitude."[4] We literally want to embrace the giver.

Reaching beyond ourselves comes naturally when we are grateful. "Gratitude can trigger the need for physical contact," writes one research team. They continue: "The opposite also seems to be true: Being hugged can trigger feelings of gratitude." In their work, they demonstrated that "friendly" and "noncompetitive" touch fostered warmth and relationship and thereby increased experiences of gratitude. Although people who did not touch felt grateful after a favor was done, people who were touched felt grateful both before and after a gift was introduced in the relationship. Touch alone raised feelings of gratitude. A touch when combined with a gift elevated feelings of gratitude even more. Hugs and touching are a result of gratitude, and increased gratitude is a result of hugs and touching. "We discovered," concluded the study authors, "that a friendly touch can promote gratitude and communal relations concurrently."[5] Without touch we can still feel grateful, but those feelings are more circumscribed than when accompanied by physical expressions of care in the friendship and community of others.

In Western societies, more people than ever live alone. In some European and North American cities, the number of single-person households nears 60 percent,[6] and social isolation tripled in the first years of the twenty-first century.[7] Although living solo is not necessarily a problem, as it points toward new patterns of potential community and the need to forge new connections, it also suggests that many people are not physically touched in friendly ways on a regular basis. Solo living along with new forms of relationships through technology have conspired to erode touch like hugging. Many observers argue our societies are awash with a loneliness epidemic, making it increasingly difficult to address a variety of collective problems from aging to economic inequality to climate change.[8]

Has social isolation also created an erosion of public gratitude?

Although gratitude has had a bit of a revival in recent years, the longer view is helpful. Use of the words "gratitude" and "thanksgiving" reached a peak around 1820 and steadily declined to a low around 2000, with similar patterns for "grateful" and "thankful."[9] Language use reveals that we are not nearly as aware of gratitude as our ancestors were. Not to wax nostalgic about it, but most nineteenth-century people lived in cultures with thicker social ties. Although there were fewer people, most resided in communities of daily physical interaction. Even with strict codes of manners and conventions like wearing gloves, I suspect people touched more in friendly (if reserved) ways. Gratitude was more readily a part of their world.

Beginning around 2000, however, something else began to occur. We started using the word "gratitude" again. Not nearly as much as in the past, but there was an uptick of use nevertheless. Are we reaching out to reclaim gratitude because we are reaching toward one another again? But where? Where in the world can we find each other in the midst of a lonely world? Can we feel grateful together?

GRATEFUL GOES VIRAL

On January 12, 2017, just days before leaving the White House, President Barack Obama surprised Vice President Joseph Biden by awarding him the Presidential Medal of Freedom with distinction.[10] After citing specific personal and political accomplishments, the president concluded, "A grateful nation thanks Vice President Joseph R. Biden, Jr., for his lifetime of service on behalf of the United States of America."

As the president placed the medal around his neck, Biden

closed his eyes as if in prayer, tears welling up, and then turned around and embraced Obama. He reached out to family and friends with hugs and kisses. Overcome with emotion, Biden stepped to the microphone and said, "This honor is far beyond what I deserve." He insisted that the award was merely a reflection of President Obama's generosity.

There was not a dry eye in the room. Or in my living room. Or, as it happened, on Facebook or Twitter.

For the next two days, the video of the event went viral, spinning off hundreds of articles and memes, all shared and shared again. Obama joked about their "bromance," while CNN referred to the award ceremony as the "best surprise party ever" and the ultimate prom-posal.[11] At heart, however, it was an unexpected, deeply felt "thank-you" party, and we were all invited via television and the Internet. More than half of my Facebook friends shared it (I actually tried to count), and most said that it made them cry. A few said that they were so distraught by the election results that they could not watch—it made them too sad. But the oddest thing about the whole event was that it was intimate and public at the same time. Watching two men express their mutual gratitude and appreciation for each other and seeing the power of gratefulness to surprise and overwhelm moved millions who were not there to feel connected to these men—as if they too were saying thank you.

Rabbi Shai Held called it the "week that Obama and Biden cried." He praised both men for displaying the sort of vulnerability that draws us together as human beings: "I am grateful to live at a time when a man—the most powerful man in the world, no less—can model what it means to let life affect him to the point where tears come."[12] A *Guardian* columnist opined, "Every time these political powerhouses become misty-eyed, they send the message that having human feelings doesn't equal incompetence."[13] Human emotions, like deep gratitude, are the opposite of incompetence: they prove the power to connect through the heart. It is not the power of an office, role, or title. Rather, it is the power of being *with* others, even millions of others, through the binding and beautiful experience of appreciation.

THE ECSTASY OF GRATITUDE

Gratitude is powerful. Theologian Lewis Smedes recalls how he felt when he realized that he had survived a life-threatening illness:

> I was seized with a frenzy of gratitude. Possessed! My arms rose straight up by themselves, a hundred-pound weight could not have held them at my side. My hands open, my fingers spread, waving, twisting, while I blessed the Lord for the almost unbearable goodness of being alive on this good earth in this good body at this present time. I was flying outside of myself, high, held in weightless lightness, as if my earthly existence needed no ground to rest in, but was hung in space with only love to keep it aloft.
>
> It was then I learned that gratitude is the best feeling I would ever have, the ultimate joy of living.[14]

As I read Smedes's account, I realized that I sat up straighter, stretched my arms wide, and took a great cleansing breath. Without intending it, I imitated him. His act of gratitude inspired me to physically move as he had moved and to empathically feel grateful. He referred to the moment as a "frenzy," but it was clearly a frenzy of wholeness and goodness. Pure joy.

In his book on happiness, social psychologist Jonathan Haidt quotes Thomas Jefferson, who actually speculated on the communal and imitative nature of beneficial emotions:

> When any . . . act of charity or of gratitude, for instance, is presented to our sight or imagination, we are deeply impressed with its beauty and feel a strong desire in ourselves of doing charitable and grateful acts also.[15]

Inspired by this Jeffersonian clue, Haidt and his researchers went on to find evidence that "people really do respond emotionally to acts of moral beauty" and that beneficial acts and feelings cause others to want to copy them. Haidt refers to this as "moral elevation," and his team demonstrated that witnessing goodness increased actual biological responses in the parasympathetic nervous system, which controls heart rate and calm breathing. Indeed, gratitude research has pointed to this same effect.[16] Gratitude, evidently, is contagious. It can be spread from heart to heart.

Haidt argues that "elevation" is generally a calming response, not the frenzy of gratitude reported by Lewis Smedes. But he also points out that that there is a related impulse: awe, or "the emotion of self-transcendence." Awe is also a dimension of gratitude. Pioneering psychologist Abraham Maslow identified moments like the one Smedes describes as "peak experiences," where the "universe is perceived as a unified whole" and the person is "flooded with feelings of wonder, awe, joy, love, and gratitude."[17] As a result, one feels more integrated, happy, and in harmony with the self and the world. This is the territory of frenzy, or ecstasy, and such experiences are also sought and imitated by others—most often through religion and spiritual practices.

Haidt studied "elevation" and Maslow studied "peak experiences" in individuals. But if gratitude elevates and is related to awe, might its imitative power be expanded beyond individuals to communities? Indeed, some social scientists have suggested that there exist "resonance patterns" whereby people find harmony and group nobility through imitation, especially in ritual and liturgy. In this state, "'I' passes unconsciously into a 'we,' 'my' becomes 'our.'"[18]

There are some fine distinctions here. For example, at many sporting events, there is a moment of appreciation for wounded veterans in the form of recognition, applause, and a song. This creates a feeling of patriotism, which, at its best, is a form of social gratitude. This act of communal thanks inspires not only good feelings toward soldier and nation; it opens the potential to imitate selflessness, noble good, and heroism.[19] Patriotic displays can—and do—result in strong emotional responses (even peak experiences) for some people. Given the nature of gratitude for one's country, that should be expected. Healthy gratitude for one's homeland, however, is not exclusive. If you are grateful for your nation, you understand that others are equally grateful for theirs. Genuine gratitude opens the heart to appreciate that people from other places feel the same.

When patriotism—the kind of gratitude that links people in a common quest for the noble good—mutates into nationalism, however, it becomes a problem. In nationalism, gratitude is the exclusive right of only some people, "us," over everyone else. It maintains that only we can be grateful because our nation is the best one and all other people are misguided when they appreciate the second-rate places where they were born. Nationalism is not about gratitude. It is about dominance. What is good cannot be shared beyond the in-group, and everyone else becomes an enemy. There is a difference between shedding a few tears during the national anthem at a baseball game and going along with the crowd at a fascist rally.

Ultimately, gratitude is an aspect of empathy. To "empathize" means to "feel in[to] or with" another, to understand and be *with* others emotionally. If you are thankful for something that cuts you off from others or sets people at odds, it may not be genuine gratitude. It may be an emotion birthed in fear or control. Gratitude connects us, even across racial, class, and national boundaries, allowing us to *feel* together. We reach out toward one another. We are elevated toward doing good. We might share the "frenzy" of gratefulness. We might find ourselves serving others or dancing in the streets.

Communal emotions are powerful. This can be frightening—and perhaps that is why we shy away from shared emotional experiences—because some feelings can cause riots, mob violence, or nationalist fervors. But there is a Sanskrit word that helps describe the positive sense of gratitude as a communal emotion: *kama muta*, "moved by love." When we are touched deeply by others, when we feel deeply with others, we experience the oneness of "love, belonging, or union—with an individual person, a family, a team, a nation, nature, the cosmos, God."[20] Profound experiences of gifts and thanks often bring forth tears, causing people to feel deeply together, even those who only witness acts of gratitude. We can recognize that we humans are communal creatures—that we can imitate one another and inspire each other toward grace and gratitude for the good of all. Like celebrating the achievement of young adults, crying with a sick pastor and his family, standing in solidarity with grieving strangers, or appreciating the friendship of two public leaders, we can feel hope and goodness together. And that should shape us in community. Gratitude. Empathy. *Kama muta*.

6

Thankful and Festive

As we travel with gratitude, and share that
feeling—like a ripple it spreads across the world.

—LARRY DVOSKIN

When I lost my job at the college, I fell into a terrible funk.
I did not know what to do with myself, and I had lost
friends and colleagues in the midst of it all. Not only had my job
disappeared, so had much of my community. Being fired is a bit
like being voted off the island. Or being sent into exile.

"You need to get out more," a friend suggested.

"What should I do?" I replied.

I really did not know. For years, my life had revolved around
religion and academics. In the wake of leaving the college, the
academic calendar no longer patterned my life. Church was

good—my new congregation was welcoming, and I was learning things there and making friends. But being freed from the constraints of evangelical expectations was disconcerting for me. Until my early thirties, my social life was shaped mostly by friendships with other evangelical Christians. I realized that I did not really know many people outside that community, and now they had essentially abandoned me. I had no idea what "secular" people did for fun. I was sheltered. Well, more like bunkered.

"Why not go with me to the wine festival?" she asked. "You like good wine. You'd love it. I promise."

I timidly agreed.

The festival was a fund-raiser for a local museum, held every year in a grove of live oak and eucalyptus trees. It was, as might be expected, a glorious Santa Barbara day, sunny and warm. Local wineries set up tables and poured generous tastings, and laughter got louder and more raucous with every glass. Strangers mingled and swayed together to the sounds of jazz. For an afternoon, I forgot about the college and everything that had happened there. I met new people, talked about food and wine, and listened to music. People were happy and not obsessed with doctrinal purity or evangelizing the world. Maybe it was the wine, but the day was light and bright and joyful. I really did not know one could enjoy life outside of church. It was everything that my stern evangelical friends warned about, the temptations of Dionysian pleasures. The mystical poet Rumi once said, "Gratitude is the wine of the soul." Whatever the truth of that, I know a wine festival pointed me toward new paths of gratitude.

It was not, of course, just the wine. It was the festivity itself, of gathering with strangers and sharing food, the sunlight, and enjoying life. I discovered that I lived in a city of festivals, of food and wine and music and theater and art, of cultures and history, of gardens and architecture and good causes. Sure, the weather was beautiful, but the people there seemed to take a particular pleasure in street fairs, parades, and all sorts of public displays of conviviality. Once, I was simply walking by a bookstore, and some street musicians began to play. People who had been strolling by stopped, listened, and started to dance on the sidewalk. Some ancient spirit of eternal festivity inhabited the place, as if the Chumash shamans continued to bless with song and dance, placing a permanent rainbow of joy across the California sky.

I had lost my job and gotten divorced, but Santa Barbara renewed my soul. The city's civic-hearted playfulness actually took me back to times in my childhood when I had experienced similar feelings of communal joy—a neighborhood Easter parade, dancing around the May Pole, a community Fourth of July picnic, a Halloween street party, harvest festivals, caroling on the main street with friends. Back when my life was not proscribed by doctrine or piety, some of the happiest times I had known happened with strangers and friends in the streets. When my friend invited me to the wine festival that day, I rediscovered communal playfulness. I remembered that festivity is central to joy.

TAKE THANKS TO THE STREETS!

Certainly, we think of such gatherings—graduations, weddings, street fairs and festivals, and harvest celebrations—as expressions of happiness. They are also expressions of a very particular kind of gratitude: the public exuberance of thanks, often in response to rites of passage or seasons of life. Graduation is a public ritual of gratitude for a child growing up and entering adult life; weddings give thanks for a marriage and the beginning of a new family; food and wine festivals originated to mark spring planting or the fall gathering in of the crop. In a real sense, the streets are the theaters of giving thanks.

As long as humans have existed, there have been such festivals. Having seen too many Hollywood films, we might easily think of these gatherings as little more than drunken orgies, like the scene in *The Ten Commandments* in which the Hebrew people reject their God to worship a golden calf instead. Although there were such wild communal events, most festivals were actually based in religious belief and celebrated the gifts of the gods toward a tribe or nation. These were festivals of gratitude, not just bacchanalia. And public celebrations of thanksgiving are an important part of the biblical story shared by Jews, Christians, and Muslims.

Professor Walter Brueggemann explains that the three great Jewish festivals of the Hebrew Bible—Passover, Pentecost, and Booths—formed a liturgical triad of celebrating God's gifts of freedom and abundance. In ancient Israel, Jews travelled to Jerusalem for each festival, leaving behind the work and responsibilities of home and village. This physical separation created an alternate space for celebration, a place at which they could arrive, as the scripture instructs "empty-handed," so that God might fill their hands with gifts. "The festivals are designed as outpourings of gratitude by Israel," insists Brueggemann, "who lives completely by the power and generosity of YHWH" (the Hebrew name for God). Indeed, the gatherings were intended to produce the emotions of humility, joy, and gratefulness to remind the Israelites that their community was grounded in generosity and gratitude, completely dependent upon the gifts of a good God.[1]

Of course, many cultures held such festivals of gratitude. The ones of ancient Israel are particularly interesting, though. In other nations, the people gathered to give their gods gifts in order that the gods might respond with gratitude to the people's praise and send them rain, an abundant harvest, or a military victory. In Israel, gratitude worked differently: God sent gifts to the people, and the people responded in gratitude and with promises to live more deeply in love and the law. Israel reversed the structure of gifts and gratitude. "In the festivals," Brueggemann says, "Israel comes to a fresh realization that its freedom is not its own work, but is a gift gladly given by YHWH. . . . Festival is the capacity to enter a way of life in which all other claims, pressures, and realities can be suspended."[2] In short, the festivals—the great communal celebrations of gratitude— modeled an alternative community, one based in abundance and joy. Festivals are a microcosm of how life should be.

"In our time and place," finishes Brueggemann, "it is a wonderment if festival can have such power and attractiveness, given pervasive complacency, self-indulgence, and individual autonomy." I do not really wonder, for I found it to be true in the streets of Santa Barbara.

GAMES AND GRATITUDE

During the autumn of 2016, baseball fans watched with a sense of astonishment as the Chicago Cubs won the World Series. Even if you were not a Cubs fan, it was hard not to appreciate the sheer magnitude of sports history that unfolded in seven nail-biting games. After 108 years of losing, the Cubs broke the fabled Curse of the Billy Goat, beat the Cleveland Indians, and reigned as baseball's champions.

The final game of the series was not played in Chicago, but in Cleveland. Thousands of Cubs fans gathered outside Chicago's Wrigley Field to share the game together. With the final out, the stadium's scoreboard lit up: "CUBS WIN." Fireworks above the park turned the night into blazing joy. Thousands of fans who gathered outside the park sang, hugged, cheered, kissed, and cried. "Grown men and women wept," reported the *Chicago Tribune*. "Fireworks lit up the sky in both the city and suburbs, while school-aged children gathered on sidewalks long after bedtime to cheer honking cars. . . . This is what it looks like when a 108-year-old dream is finally realized."[3] People took to the streets with a celebration three generations in the making. "It was," said one young fan on behalf of myriad others, "the greatest night of my life."

Two days later, the team joined their fans on the streets. The city hosted a parade and a rally in Grant Park, and the jubilation continued, with as many as five million people lining streets and showing up at the event. A local television station reported, "Cubs World Series Celebration Ranks as the 7th Largest Gathering in Human History!" positioning the Chicago victory party between the pope's 2015 visit to the Philippines and the 1970 funeral of Egypt's President Nasser in historic magnitude.[4] The more restrained *Chicago Tribune* also said that crowds were large, but the numbers may have been "exaggerated" due to "runaway enthusiasm."

In the months following the victory, there were fewer people dancing in Chicago streets, but enthusiasm did not abate. The celebrations gave way to another form of communal bonding: gratitude. As the *Washington Post* reported:

> The Cubs' players and staff have grown accustomed to a strange phenomenon. Everywhere they go people come up to them with stories—of a late father, a grandfather, a mother, a grandmother, a brother, or a sister who was the biggest Cubs fan of them all. The World Series title would have meant so much to them. Almost uniformly, the interaction ends with two words: thank you.
>
> "It's a lot of gratitude," says Cubs manager Joe Maddon. "It's the same refrain from everybody. For the most part, they don't want an autograph or a picture. They just want to shake your hand and say thank you."[5]

Sports and gratitude do not often show up in the same sentence. When we think of raucous emotions at a sporting event, rowdy crowds, perhaps coming close to riot, and on occasion violence come to mind. The emotions let loose during games seem birthed in the strivings of competition, unrelated to the genteel strains of thanksgiving. But sports and communal emotion go together. "For most people in the world today," claims journalist Barbara Ehrenreich, "the experience of collective ecstasy is likely to be found, if it is found at all, not in a church or at a concert or rally but at a sports event."[6]

Yet "ecstasy" depends on relief and release. In giant stadiums, relief and release can be the result of beer sales. But relief and release come from other sources as well—relief from no longer being losers, release from the curse that haunted a team. Relief and release are tied to appreciation—for a lucky break, the stars aligning, the talent and grit of the players. And not just for fans, but for players as well. A pitcher who cannot seem to put away an inning and might lose the game suddenly focuses and strikes out three batters. As he walks off the field, he looks to the heavens and says, "Thank you." The crowd cheers their appreciation. A tennis player behind in her set rallies for the win. As she scores the final point, she falls to her knees with gratitude, and spectators breathe that moment of thanksgiving with her. The communal experience of sports is often linked to gratitude, a festal ecstasy that is part beer and part praise.

Thanksgiving and sports have often mixed. No doubt those ancient Israelites kicked around a few balls while they waited their turn to sacrifice lambs in thanks to YHWH at the temple in Jerusalem. In America, the first Thanksgiving football game was played on November 30, 1873, when Princeton and Yale faced one another in Hoboken, New Jersey. The whole thing proved such a huge success that the schools moved the Thanksgiving game to New York City, where, in a single decade, attendance grew from five to an astonishing forty thousand fans, leading reporters to claim that it was "the greatest sporting event . . . this country has to show."[7] The Princeton-Yale game was accompanied by a massive parade on Broadway, complete with tailgating, albeit in horse-drawn carriages, and inebriated students. Thus, the original New York Thanksgiving Day parade was not a commercial celebration of department-store fame (that would come later in 1924). Rather, New York's first such parade offered harvest thanks and celebrated pigskin.

In a recent academic study, Professor Lung Hung Cheng discovered that athletes with a strong sense of gratitude had a higher sense of personal well-being and team satisfaction: "Grateful athletes are more satisfied with their team and over-all lives." The more thankful a player is for training, mentors, and other players, the more supported and successful the player feels. This support, in turn, builds persistence and confidence and connects individual players to a community of teammates.[8] Grateful people play together better.

That, of course, is the real point. Sports can be serious business (yes, real business, the money-making kind), it can be a competition, and it can be worship. At its core, however, sport is organized play—a game. And it turns out that play and grati-tude are linked. Mary Beth Sammons, coauthor of *The Grateful Life*, recalls how she struggled as her father and mother passed away—not quickly—but over six long years of illness and mul-tiple hospitalizations. At the same time, she was also helping to raise her three-year-old granddaughter. She unexpectedly dis-covered that playing with the toddler opened the door to healing gratitude. "Play opened the path from brokenness to the search for light in every corner of every moment I was experiencing," she remembers. "It helped me tap into a new level of conscious-ness. Play unplugged my fear, letting me shed tears of sorrow and joy, and gave me hope and reverence for the precious mo-ments spent at my parents' sides."[9]

And how did this help her toward gratefulness? By provid-ing physical relief from the weariness of hospital routine, by re-leasing her to remember her parents' rich lives, and by opening up new ways of connecting with them and their memory. She writes of playing with her grandchild:

Play shifted my lens. It filled me with memories of my childhood and spending times just like this with both my parents, who introduced me to the sheer pleasure of holding a good book and entering a new world through its pages. I was grateful for parents who let me gather my friends and build a tree house in our backyard. . . . I remembered with thankfulness my mom driving me and my friends to the skating rink, where most winters we practically lived all day, racing around the track and sipping hot chocolate. . . .

Through play, I could let go with love of the fact that my parents would no longer physically be a part of my life. But I learned that they would live on in the books they had taught me to love, [and] in the spirit of playfulness.[10]

Play is sports and play is festivity. Although not completely impossible to do, we generally do not play alone. Even if no team is around, we might play with a dog, with a toddler, with another friend. But play does not isolate. We play together.

And play leads us to a different place. After the stressful American election in 2016 and the first months of the Trump presidency, my husband looked at me over dinner one night and said, "I can't wait for baseball season. Baseball is pretty much the only thing that can help right now."

We live in Washington, D.C., where politics is always in your face, where national news is local news. There is no escape. Except through our sports teams, like the Washington Nationals. My husband is a fanatical fan, one who lives in a mixture of gratitude and eternal hope. Baseball is not a distraction—it is more of a religion. It saves him. He does not just watch games; rather, he "plays" them with his team. True sports fans are never merely spectators; they participate. They breathe and live with and for the game. Professor Joseph Price, who has written on the Super Bowl, sees play as a spiritual experience:

> It's possible to take play seriously, and it's possible for faith to be an act of play. And play is an exercise basically of the spirit. Watch children in a playground at a park, their spirits soar. And isn't that what we aspire to cultivate in faith communities, to have the adults' spirits soar? Perhaps we need elements of play in worship, in sport.[11]

Play is an exercise basically of the spirit. On the playground and in the stands. If that is a road map for faith communities, then it is also a life-giving way beyond the walls of church or synagogue. Public playfulness and public thanksgiving go hand-in-glove. Sports are so much more than winning. Our stadiums, or perhaps local bars where people (who cannot afford expensive tickets) gather to cheer on a beloved team, might well be our most public arenas of gratitude.[12] When we play, when we cheer on our team, we are performing thanks. Games and gratitude go together.

THE EUCHARIST

Another communal place where imbibing and praise come together in gratitude is in church, in a ritual celebration called the Eucharist, where people share bread and wine with each other. Of course, wine combined with religion is nothing new. Since the beginning of human history, frenzied worshippers have poured out libations before their gods, often in great festivals resembling spiritual orgies. In these celebrations, people celebrated wine and harvest as they sang, played, and danced in the streets, hoping such ecstasy would please the gods and remind them to send food and wine next year too.

Ancient Romans were good at it. So when word got out that Christians held feasts of bread and wine, their pagan neighbors were not shocked. What the Romans found surprising was that the Christians did it in secret, leading their critics to wonder if the Jesus festival was so lurid that Christians had to do it behind closed doors. Surely, they thought, whatever Eucharist was, it must be immoral.

"Eucharist" is the word that Episcopalians, Catholics, Orthodox Christians, some Lutherans, and some Presbyterians use to refer to the meal others call the Lord's Supper or Communion. It is the central ritual of Christian community, considered the most sacred moment of Sunday worship. Participants eat bread and drink wine—in what most call a "sacrament"—to reenact the final meal Jesus shared with his disciples on the night before he died. The word "Eucharist" is from the Greek *eukharistia*, meaning "thanksgiving" or "gratitude." It is a compound term derived from the Greek words *eu*, for "well," and *kharis*, for "favor" or "grace." Thus, Eucharist, that is, "gratitude," means "well-favored" or "good grace."

Bread is blessed and shared, a reminder that food is a gift from God, the gift that gives life to our bodies; wine is blessed and shared, a reminder that drink is a gift from God, a gift that gives joy to our souls. God gives good gifts of favor and grace; the people receive and respond with promises of faithfulness and thanksgiving. The Eucharist does not really resemble pagan harvest celebrations. There, the emphasis is on pleasing the gods and imploring them to send more bread and wine next year. Rather, the Christian celebration echoes those ancient Hebrew festivals in which the Jews recognized and received God's gifts of abundance and, with humility, returned gratefulness. No need to please or plead, for God's gift is all of creation—and these gifts surround all people through all time. God does not need to be convinced to give or begged to send favor. But human beings need to be reminded that abundance is the nature of existence. The Jews went to Jerusalem two or three times a year to remember this and give thanks for it.

Christians go to their congregations weekly or monthly to do the same—to feast upon (that is, have a "festival" of) gratefulness. The Jewish and Christian settings are different, but the biblical story of abundance and thanks is pretty much the same. That is what church is intended to be: a festive community dependent on gifts of abundance. Everything is a gift. Bread is a gift; wine is a gift; life and joy are gifts. No one can ever pay them back. God never withholds. All we can do is receive—in awe of such favor and grace—say thank you to the Giver, and then "pay it forward" with humble service to others. Just like the Jews. But, for Christians, the story is mediated through Jesus. Eucharist. Gratitude. Thanksgiving.

On occasion, I have heard Christians speak of "taking the Eucharist." "Oh," someone might say, "I haven't been to church for a while. I need to go and take the Eucharist." This colloquialism comes from Jesus's words reported in the Gospel of Matthew: "While they were eating, Jesus took a loaf of bread, and after blessing it he broke it, gave it to the disciples, and said,

'Take, eat; this is my body'" (26:26). So people "take" the bread. But how do you "take" a gift? One definition of "take" is as a synonym for "steal," for example, when we "take" something illegally or stealthily, something not belonging to or intended for us. Or maybe we take something so someone else cannot. If we take something, we make it ours, we own it. Taking is so wrapped up with status, power, and privilege, with notions of entitlement and economics, that it just does not seem to relate abundance and gratefulness.

Interestingly enough, the Greek word is *labete*, which is translated "to take" but also means "to receive." When Jesus handed bread to his friends, he said, "Receive, feast"—receive, not take. To receive gifts and to give thanks is *the* story of faith. To shift the word removes any connotation of economic exchange and ownership and reaffirms that the Eucharist is a free gift. Grace and favor are for all, to all, and with the whole world. Receiving, not taking, is the very meaning of our shared humanity, and it is the thread of community.

At the center of Christian experience is a gift of abundance (Jesus actually referred to it as "abundant life"; John 10:10) that is received with humility and calls a people to respond with gratitude and faithfulness. Thus, giving thanks is the primary communal emotion of Christianity. Not every church makes this point through the ritual of the Eucharist. Some do so through more ecstatic means, like the Pentecostal service that made me uncomfortable when I was a teenager, and others do so through music and hymns or public prayer.

It can, however, be difficult to give public thanks. In liturgical churches, the Eucharist is often seen as private, an act in which individuals go forward in a single line or kneel at an altar in a sort of spiritual cocoon not so much to delight in the generosity of God as to beg for forgiveness for their personal sins; here the Eucharist is less about receiving than it is about penitential pleading. In that Pentecostal service, the preacher had to call people out to give thanks. I have worshipped in many traditional churches where the public prayers were full of requests for healing and justice, but when the pastor asked for thanksgivings, an eerie silence filled the sanctuary. Even though gratitude is the heart of faith, Christians seem to have a hard time getting there. At least in public.

About a decade ago, journalist Cathleen Falsani sought an interview with her favorite poet, Nobel laureate Seamus Heaney. She wanted to ask him about spirituality. But Heaney, who was born a Catholic in Protestant Northern Ireland, was reluctant to address the subject. He had drifted away from his childhood Irish Catholicism, but his poetry reveals a grounded soul with a keen awareness of the sacred. Falsani was curious as to what he thought about faith. Heaney declined to answer, saying that he was "woefully inarticulate" when it came discussing such matters. However, he did something else. He replied by sending her a poem, one that spoke to his sense of spirit and that revealed the Eucharist as gift and gratitude:

> Like everybody else, I bowed my head
> during the consecration of the bread and wine,
> lifted my eyes to the raised host and raised chalice,
> believed (whatever it means) that a change occurred.
>
> I went to the altar rails and received the mystery
> on my tongue, returned to my place, shut my eyes
>   fast, made

an act of thanksgiving, opened my eyes and felt
time starting up again.[13]

Even when one leaves church behind, the Eucharist remains,
always holding out the mystery of gift. Life and joy for all. Receive and give thanks. The world made new.

POLITICAL EXUBERANCE

Having been to political conventions, I can testify that they are
theaters of play and communal exuberance. There is nothing
else quite like the balloon drop when a favorite candidate se-
cures a presidential bid—when emotions overflow and hopes
run high with dreams of victory. Politics is another arena where
we experience communal gratitude. But there it gets a lot more
complicated.

On January 20, 2009, I was speaking at a conference on
St. Simon's Island in Georgia. St. Simon's is beautiful, but I was
distressed about being away from my home outside of Washington. My house was full of guests, friends, and relatives attending
President Obama's inauguration, and I was not there.

The conference attracted mostly progressive Christians and
had been scheduled long before Barack Obama's historic election. We were meeting in a conference center that did not have
televisions in all the rooms, and I suspected that many would be
disappointed to miss the inauguration. So I asked the organizers
if they could stream the event live into the massive auditorium
where we gathered for the keynote speeches.

They seemed reluctant. The vast majority of the eight hundred attendees, one leader admitted, surely supported the new

president, but there would be a few who did not vote for him and might be offended. I pressed on, however, and the other speaker joined in my request. Thus, on Inauguration Day, I watched President Obama take the oath of office with several hundred liberal Southerners. There was a lot of crying and cheering. We knew we stood on slave ground, not far from a spot where some slave cabins still survived. Most of those at the conference grew up during segregation, and some had worked for civil rights throughout the South. For them, watching a black man become president was cathartic. Many commented how grateful they were that we could be together to celebrate and how much they appreciated sharing the emotions and excitement in community. Even though we were far from Washington, we made our own inauguration party right there, on the watery shores of the old Confederacy.

Some of the organizing team, however, did not seem entirely happy with me for having made the request. I imagine they heard from the attendees who did not support the new president. One person pointedly refused to speak to me for the rest of the event. I felt terrible for the rest of the week. It was, in a word, awkward.

The moral of the story? One person's ecstatic celebration can be another person's greatest fear. When politics comes into the mix, things get dicey.

In the United States, we live in a time when it is easier to celebrate a baseball team from another city than it is to celebrate a presidential inauguration. There is a reason for this, one that is quite important to how and where we celebrate together. In the case of a sports team, we are usually celebrating something more than just winning. Other than the people in Chicago who wanted to win, Americans celebrated the Cubs because they had been losers and they became a jaw-dropping, great baseball team. We cheered their story, their history, their talent—we were thankful that even some who were unlucky for a hundred years could rise above it and achieve their dream. We loved their story. And unless you were a die-hard Cleveland Indians fan, you could be grateful for it.

On St. Simon's, I am sure there were some conservatives who thought we liberals were thankful that "we" won and that "they" lost, that we were celebrating a winner in order to kick a loser. I was not thinking about winning or losing. I was grateful for a story, a long American story about race and oppression that seemed to be coming to an end in January 2009 with the election of a black president. It was like cheering the Cubs. It was not that Republicans lost; it was the overwhelming beauty of the achievement itself and the new possibilities for America's future.

Political gratitude, however, is rarely about the beauty of the thing. It is too often about partisan power and control. Mary Jo Leddy explains it this way:

> If we tend to imagine power as a pie, either very big or very little, then we tend to think in terms of some having more and others less. One person's gain is another's loss. Where dissatisfaction reigns supreme, as it does in our culture, then the scene is set for a conflict over the pie. Only the whole pie will suffice; nothing else will satisfy.[14]

Thus, the kinds of celebrations that result from "pie grabbing" breed resentment, the exact opposite of communal gratitude. Although a political rally might be cause for thanks for true believers, those outside the circle see such an event as an insult or threat. If political events focus on a single individual, like a candidate or a head of state, they can easily become authoritarian spectacles rather than true communal celebrations. It is very easy to turn partisan exuberance into manipulation, even violence.[15] The "test" of any political event is its result: Does the communal celebration bring out good civic character or ill? Who appears—the better angels of our nature or the demons within?

An inauguration is not intended to be a partisan rally. It is intended to be a festival of thanksgiving for democracy and the nonviolent transfer of power. It is meant to celebrate a process and a people and give thanks for a land. That intent has been lost, perhaps because it was a bit of a myth in the first place or perhaps because our practice of politics has become more malevolent in recent years.

Leddy's remark should haunt us: *where dissatisfaction reigns supreme.* . . . The fact that we have lost the binding power of civic festivity is disturbing. Ingratitude is a perpetual state of dissatisfaction. Ingratitude is about what we do not have, what we feel we deserve, what we can never get, or what keeps us from our rightful part of the pie. Ingratitude and genuine civic festivity are deadly enemies. If we cannot play together, if we are not thankful in the common arena, we cannot be a good team. Public ingratitude threatens rather than invites, isolates rather than unites. As a result, we lose the experience of shared communal joy.

Psychologists have demonstrated that feeling grateful is good for the heart, that gratitude strengthens health and well-being. If that is true for individuals, it is true for communities and countries as well. To feel grateful together moves us from "me" and "my" political opinions toward "we" and the good of "our" community. Communal gratitude might heal our civic heart, putting us on a path toward a new future of national emotional health and well-being. We—that is, those of us in divided, discouraged, and dissatisfied Western societies—could use a big-scale gratitude intervention, not in the form of some solemn scold, but in the guise of a global street party. Times are difficult, yes, but we have so much to be grateful for. Our lives really are surrounded by gifts. We need to let loose in thanks.

According to Barbara Ehrenreich, instead of partisan rallies in our politics, we are in need of more civic festivals:

> The capacity for collective joy is encoded into us almost as deeply as the capacity for the erotic love of one human for another. We can live without it, as most of us do, but only at the risk of succumbing to the solitary nightmare of depression. Why not reclaim our distinctively human heritage as creatures who can generate their own ecstatic pleasures out of music, color, feasting, and dance?[16]

Why not? Why not rediscover gratitude through play?

THANKSGIVING

So how can we reclaim gratitude in our communal settings? If gratitude is contagious, it is our duty to spread it. Perhaps it starts by attending a local sporting event, a citywide festival, or a block party celebrating summer. More than anything else, though, I want to reclaim Thanksgiving as our major festival of gratefulness. In the United States, Thanksgiving currently suffers from two major problems: it is relegated to the status of a private family celebration and it serves as the commercial kick-off for Christmas.

Other than providing us with a day off from work (a public holiday) and engendering a few civic proclamations (ignored by most), Thanksgiving has largely moved from the public sphere to the domestic one. Generally, we celebrate in intimate groups, typically family, in our own homes with our own feasts and watch games on our own televisions. Some of the privatization has emerged, no doubt, because of a certain awkwardness associated with the holiday—the picture of happy Natives feeding grateful Pilgrims just does not square with the historical record. Nor do the nostalgic Norman Rockwell images of a family patriarch overseeing a happy nuclear family at a table fit with the experiences of most American families today. Without a larger sense of story and not knowing how to move past the myths we once lived by, we retreat into our private spheres and make the best of a day off—and stuff ourselves with turkey.

With regard to the second problem, today Thanksgiving in America is lost in the consumerist rush to Christmas. Not so long ago, stores closed in a grateful pause that allowed shoppers and sellers to breathe before the December holiday. Now, however, you get a couple hours to gobble down the meal with the relatives before you rush out for holiday discounts. Huge crowds gather not to play, but to be the first in line at Walmart. This is not the ecstasy of gratitude—it is the agony of scarcity. Instead of giving thanks for abundance, we push to the front of the queue to make sure we get ours before anyone else beats us to it. Consumer Thanksgiving is more a zero-sum game than a celebration of bounty. Advertisers remind us that supplies are limited. In what has become an orgy of "I'll get mine," often someone dies in the struggle for a must-have toy or cheap smart phone.

But Thanksgiving is still there, no matter how ignored, privatized, or corrupted it may be. There are parades (which need not be commercials for Christmas), feasts (some of which are provided by service groups and religious communities), and sports. If the surveys are right—that 80 percent of us experience gratitude on a regular basis—why not celebrate that? Gratitude, evidently, is something we share. We might even give thanks for the binding power of thanks! Gratefulness is not partisan, exclusive, or even necessarily religious. Indeed, one of my favorite Thanksgiving blessings comes from Adam Lee, an atheist:

> As we come together to share this meal, let us first remember how it came to us and be thankful to the people who made it possible.
>
> This food was born from the bounty of the Earth, in warm sunlight, rich earth, and cool rain.
>
> May it nourish us, in body and mind, and provide us with the things that are good for living.
>
> We are grateful to those who cultivated it, those who harvested it, those who brought it to us, and those who prepared it.
>
> May its consumption bring about the pleasures of friendship, love, and good company.

And as we partake of this food in each other's company, as what was once separate from all of us becomes part of each of us, may we also remember what we have in common and what brings us all together.

May this sharing of food foster peace and understanding among us, may it bring us to the recognition that we depend on each other for all the good we can ever hope to receive, and that all the good we can hope to accomplish rests in helping others in turn.

May it remind us that as we reach out to others to brighten their lives, so are our lives brightened in turn.[17]

These words also serve to remind us what we can celebrate together: food, the bounty of the earth, the gifts of life and work, the pleasure of relationships, the real unity of community, peace and interdependence, and a call to serve others as we have been served. We celebrate a day when we can turn history on its head and say that Thanksgiving is not about colonists taking from Native peoples, but about the abundance of a beautiful land, a land bountiful enough for all, that it is a day marking humility, forgiveness, and appreciation. These things are worth celebrating. Heck, they are worth shouting from rooftops, singing about, and whooping it up in the streets.

But not only does the American Thanksgiving need renewal—Thanksgiving needs to go global. The world does not need just an American Thanksgiving, or a Canadian Thanksgiving, or a Japanese Thanksgiving, or any number of other national Thanksgiving Days.[18] The whole planet could use a day to say thank you. Maybe on September 21, World Gratitude Day, which was started in Hawaii in 1965 and has since been adopted by the United Nations, but is not yet universally celebrated. It is a great idea, one that is growing, and certainly one whose time has come.

Thanksgiving—everywhere!—should have fireworks, bands, street parties, and games—football, soccer, basketball, what have you. It should not be just a day on a calendar, but a genuine global festival. Let prayers and benedictions from Christians, Jews, Muslims, Buddhists, Hindus, Wiccans, humanists, agnostics, and atheists sound: "THANK YOU!" Let's have a great big global celebration to recognize the gift of life we share, to respond with humble thanks, and to recommit ourselves to serve nature and neighbor. Let it be a day of gratitude from every corner of the earth.

Let's inaugurate that.

IV

We: Ethics
Community and Politics

If you're grateful, you're not fearful, and if
you're not fearful, you're not violent. If you're
grateful, you act out of a sense of enough and
not of a sense of scarcity, and you are willing
to share. If you are grateful, you are enjoying
the differences between people, and you are
respectful to everybody, and that changes this
power pyramid under which we live.

—DAVID STEINDL-RAST

The Grateful Society

May we not keep our blessings,
but give them away.

—THOM M. SHUMAN

On January 21, 2017, I woke early and got ready to take the Metro from my home in northern Virginia to downtown Washington, D.C. For months, a single word had blocked out the day before on my calendar: "Inauguration." My daughter and I had planned to celebrate Hillary Clinton's becoming America's first female president. Instead, because of a sad and unexpected election result, we stayed home on Inauguration Day. One day later, and alone because my daughter went back to college, I journeyed into the city for an alternate event: the Women's March.

My husband dropped me off at the subway station nearest our house, something he does for me on a fairly regular basis.

"Wow. Look at all those buses," he exclaimed as he pointed to a convoy of charters with North Carolina license plates.

"And look at that line!" I replied, directing his attention toward the entrance where more than a hundred people waited. "I've never seen so many people here."

"I wonder if it is like this at every stop?" he said. "It's so early. It doesn't even start for hours. Could be a big day. I bet this will be something." He pulled up to the "Kiss and Ride" and, dutifully obeying the sign, pecked me on the cheek. "Have fun! Call when you want to be picked up."

I hopped out, took a bright fuchsia crocheted hat from my coat pocket, put it on my head, and joined a group of women who were carrying signs and wearing identical headgear.

With the exception of the pink hats and the protest signs, the metro car resembled a scene from rush hour at the Tokyo subway. On the train, there was barely a place to stand. When we disembarked at L'Enfant Plaza, thousands coursed through the station.

I had arranged to meet some friends—mostly clergywomen—in front of the National Museum of the American Indian. Although the crowd was already larger than any I had ever seen (and it would grow into one of the largest protest gatherings in history), I arrived first at the meet-up location. The patio was already jammed with marchers. I worried that my friends would not find me, as I was just one pink hat among thousands.

I looked around and realized that the museum had placed huge boulders around its entrance as (I suspected) both a landscape design and security feature. I scrambled up on the rocks. From there, I could both survey the crowd and be seen.

I waited. Standing on the boulders eventually worked.

Across the growing crowd, hands waved in recognition! My friends navigated through the throng to the rocks. There was no place to stand on the patio, so they joined me on that artificial mount (and the concrete bench at its base). We greeted each other with hugs and tears. Finally, one said, "We brought the signs!"

She passed them out to the dozen or so of us who made up this small Christian band, with our pink hats, ordination stoles, and clergy collars. A few other women who were pastors saw us and joined the party, and she gave them signs too. I looked at the placard she handed me, a piece of black cardboard with rounded white letters that read:

Blessed are the poor—Matthew 5

The Beatitudes! Our signs were Jesus's words from the Sermon on the Mount in the New Testament. I laughed with delight as I read them all:

Blessed are the peacemakers
Blessed are those who mourn
Blessed are the merciful
Blessed are the hungry

Not only were there signs bearing the actual words from the Bible, but my friends had added a few special updated Beatitudes for the day:

Blessed are the women
Blessed are the uninsured

Blessed are the immigrants
Blessed are the LGBTQ

We were marching with the Beatitudes.

Or not. Because we were stuck. The crowd had so filled in that it was difficult to move, much less march.

We stayed up on the rocks, wearing pink hats and clerical collars and holding up blessings as women slowly filed by below.

"Yeah! Blessed are the poor!" a voice shouted from the crowd.

"I'm mourning *a lot* right now," yelled another. "I must be really blessed!"

And more replies: "God bless the immigrants!" "Jesus welcomes everybody!" "Blessed are the protestors!" "Even politicians would be blessed if they passed single-payer health insurance!" "Blessed are the working mothers!"

Some pointed at the signs, commenting: "Look, the church is here!" "Who knew that Christians would show up at a march like this?" Others seemed surprised to see clergy: "Blessed are women preachers!" And surprised by the presence of collared women, more than a few marchers stopped to talk and pray.

My mind wandered back to the New Testament, to an ancient hillside in Galilee, where Jesus had stood just above the crowds and uttered these blessings for the first time. Looking out at the poor, the weak, the oppressed, women, and slaves, he preached his radical Sermon on the Mount, proclaiming the promise of a new society. Although the words were so familiar to me because I had heard them all my life, when I stood up on the rocks in the middle of the Women's March, I realized that Jesus's sermon added up to one thing: "Blessed are all of you who are disregarded by the powerful, for you are God's beloved community."

Jesus blessed history's losers. No wonder people all those years ago had listened. No wonder they remembered and wrote it down. No wonder it is still so powerful two millennia later. The blessings were protest against injustice.

I looked down from the artificial hillside, and my heart moved as I watched the crowds. I held my sign up higher and shouted, "Blessed are the poor!" Some women yelled back, "Blessed are the poor!" And others cheered. Yes, they cheered the Beatitudes.

And tears came. The day before, I had cried because I was afraid and sad. But on this day I cried because of blessings. For the first time in two months, I felt grateful.

GRATITUDE IS AN emotion we experience as individuals, and we can each practice gratitude as a personal ethic, the foundation of a good life. Yet gratitude is inherently social; it always connects us as individuals to others. Communal gratitude looks and feels wonderful when festivity, play, and ecstasy draw us together. Just as personal gratefulness comprises both emotions and ethics, so does communal gratitude. The grateful-feeling community can—and should—lead to a grateful society. Feeling grateful is not only play, but it can be a form of politics. Gratitude is joy, and gratitude is justice.

True gratitude, real gratefulness, the kind of transformative thanksgiving that makes all things new, cannot be quiet in the face of injustice. If we embrace the sort of gratitude that changes our individual lives, it will revolutionize our political lives as well. We move from a personal ethic of gratefulness toward a public one. The "me" of gratitude must extend to the "we" of gratitude as an ethic, a vision of community based on habits and practices of grace and gifts, of cultivating a wide field of vision and deepening our awareness of humility and blessing, of setting tables and sharing food for all. Gratitude is not merely resilience. Gratitude is resistance too.

It is time for all of us to join the resistance.

BLESSED COMMUNITY

As I experienced that day at the Women's March, blessings and gratitude are intimately connected. Few of us are naturally thankful for things that appear to curse us! We give thanks for friends, health, provision, and love: blessings. We are blessed, and we are grateful.

But what are blessings? The English noun "blessing" means "gift from God" and is derived from the verb "to bless," "to hallow, or to make holy." Eventually, "bless" became associated with "bliss," meaning merriment, happiness, and favor. Thus, "blessing" came to be used in two senses—as both a sacred gift and something that makes one happy. Gifts and gratitude are always of a piece. Blessings and thanks go together.

The Beatitudes, however, can be confusing. Few give thanks for poverty, hunger, or grief as Jesus did in his sermon. Most contemporary people have a very different idea of what makes a blessed life. *Blessed are the rich, for they own the best stuff. Blessed are the sexy and glamorous, for everyone desires them. Blessed are the powerful, for they shall control the kingdoms of the earth. Blessed are those who get everything they ever wanted; they alone will be satisfied. Blessed are the famous, for their reward is eternal life.* Money, beauty, power, achievement, and fame—we hold these things in esteem. If only we had them, or just one of them, we would be blessed. We have forgotten the meaning of the word, identifying it mostly with material things and consumer goods.

The Greek word for "blessing" ascribed to Jesus in the Beatitudes is *makarios*, which means both "happiness" and "favor." A few Bible translations actually replace "blessed" with "happy," reading "Happy are the poor" and "Happy are the hungry." To understand blessings as mere happiness, however, often results in a strange view of blessings: it seems to say poverty or starvation is a gift, and we should be happy to have it.

The alternate sense, however, opens a new understanding of the relationship between blessing and gratitude. Blessing is not just happiness, but favor. In the Christian scriptures, the word specifically means God's favor, often called "grace" or "abundance." "Favored are the poor" or "Gifted are the poor" would be equally valid ways of making sense of *makarios*.

The sense of the Beatitudes is *not* "If you are poor, God will bless you" (as a sort of consolation prize) or "If you do nice things for the poor, God will bless you." Nor is it "Be happy *for* poverty." Instead, "Blessed are the poor" could be read, "God privileges the poor." If you are poor, you are favored by God. God's gifts are with you. This would have shocked Jesus's hearers on that day long ago. Blessing was beyond the reach of everyday people. "The blessed" in Greek actually became interchangeable with "the gods" and "the elite" and meant something like "those worthy of honor." Thus, the "the blessed" were the big shots of the ancient world, the upper crust, those who lived above all the worries of normal existence. The poor, "the losers," had to live with shame.[1] Even back then, the blessed were the rich, not the poor.

In the Roman Empire, the world in which the Beatitudes were first preached, people believed that the emperor was uniquely blessed and all blessings flowed through him—the one worthy of honor—to everyone else. The richer and more powerful you were, the more valor and virtue you possessed, the closer you were to the emperor at the top of the social hierarchy, the more blessed you were, and the more blessings you could (if you chose to) bestow on those beneath you. When Jesus said, "Blessed are the poor," he overturned the politics of blessing. He preached that blessings were more than happiness. They were a social vision. God gives gifts to *everyone*, but especially to the vulnerable and those at the bottom of society. Gifts are not only for the few, but wildly distributed for all. And the people at the bottom? The losers? God's favor resides with them. God has uniquely blessed them.

What is the proper response to gifts? Gratitude. Blessing is an invitation to give thanks.

We also get something else wrong about blessing. We tend to think of it as directed to individuals. In this amazing sermon about blessings, however, Jesus addressed a crowd. Of his nine blessings, seven are plural—"they" and "theirs"—and only two are singular. Jesus was more concerned about a blessed community than blessing people one by one. This is not about *my* blessings, but about *ours*. At the end of the sermon, Matthew reports: "Now when Jesus had finished saying these things, the crowds were astounded at his teaching" (7:28).

I bet they were thankful too, for a blessed community is a grateful community. They started as a crowd, and the way opened for them to become a society formed by gratitude.

Haunted by Rome

Through human history, gratitude has been built into society. We human beings do things for others who do things for us. "Reciprocity," claims Jonathan Haidt, "is a deep instinct; it is the basic currency of social life."[2] Doing favors and repaying favors—the most foundational definition of gratitude—forms the core of familial, tribal, and political relationships, forging connections of trust, debt, cooperation, and connection through large groups of people. In other words, gratitude is indelibly communal.

Communities are not just random groupings. They are the purposeful forms that organize human life and work. We structure community around ideas of power, protection, production, and obligation, often linking those things with cosmology and religion. Gratitude is not, therefore, a free-floating emotion or ethic. It exists within these communal structures, and our experience of gratitude is profoundly influenced by social and political arrangements.

Although more than fifteen hundred years have passed since its end, the structures of the ancient Roman Empire still haunt Western societies. This is especially true in relation to gratitude. Politically, Rome was a hierarchical pyramid, with the emperor on top as its focal point of unity and faith. He was the ultimate benefactor of the Roman world, the very model of generosity, justice, provision, and civic welfare. Everything good descended from him to the lower ranks of people—nobles, soldiers, citizens, merchants, peasants, foreigners, conquered peoples, and finally, slaves. If you had food, it was because of Rome's largesse, embodied by the emperor. If you owned land, it was because Rome gave it to you. If you were happy, it was because Rome offered peace. A system of gifts and tribute, a structure of patronage, held Rome together.

The emperor bestowed gifts, and all his beneficiaries returned their gratitude in the form of taxes, tithes, tributes, honor, loyalty, public works, and return favors. "Gratitude was not merely warm feeling toward the benefactor," writes historical theologian Peter Leithart, "but reciprocal service and benefaction. Benefits imposed a debt on the recipient that had to be discharged through a return of service or benefit."[3] This hierarchical structure of gratitude with its required reciprocity was the glue of ancient Roman society and politics.[4]

Since economic benefits flowed down, the members of each social class took a share for themselves and left less for the classes below. By the time benefits reached the bottom rung of society, they were paltry and thinly distributed. Yet the lower down you were in the social structure, the less you received, but the more you owed to those above you. Gifts flowed down. Gratitude repayment flowed upward. In the same way that members of each social class skimmed benefits flowing down, they also took their share of tribute and taxes as payback made its way back up the pyramid. In order for the emperor to receive his proper portion (and everyone to take theirs), taxes were inordinately high on the poor. In contemporary terms, gratitude's payback was regressive and often created huge financial debts for the lower classes. "Debts of gratitude" were monetary debts, not only social ones. The poorer you were, the more you were required to return to your benefactors. In this system, ingratitude was a political and economic act—to refuse to pay or return a favor was treason. The Roman philosopher Seneca insisted that nothing was more "harmful to society" than not being grateful.[5] Ingratitude was "the cardinal social and political sin in the Graeco-Roman world."[6]

Ancient Romans could not imagine an empire without gratitude. But their idea of gratitude—of repayment for imperial favor—was embedded in the structure of their politics. Obligatory reciprocity was the fabric of society. Gratitude was not a feeling. It was a political requirement.

Even after the fall of the Roman Empire, this structure continued in the form of medieval feudalism. It developed into a complex system of quid pro quo, "tit for tat," "I do this for you, you do that for me," with devastating social consequences involving everything from destructive land practices and unjust laws to wars of insult and personal revenge. Europeans struggled with the ghost of Roman benefaction for centuries. In the seventeenth and eighteenth centuries new options emerged, however; as philosophers and politicians imagined a new system of contracts and chosen obligations in politics and business, they banished gratitude to the private sphere of domestic relations (see discussion in Chapter 1). Instead of order through benefactions and tributes, public life would be governed by covenants, contracts, democratic process, and the rule of law.

Gratitude was thus pushed into the domestic sphere, where it flourished. Given the chance, women reshaped gratitude as a structure of emotions, relationships, and manners. Elaborate, yes, and with pitfalls surely. But women subverted the hierarchical structure of gratitude and turned it toward virtues of love and festivity. In the male-dominated public sphere, however, patronage and payback kept sneaking back in—mostly through business.

Eventually, commercial interests overtook democratic ideals of civic life, and business brought with it brokers, patrons, deal makers, and tit-for-tat arrangements. As corporate interests grew, gratitude mutated into lobbying (a profession based on obligatory reciprocity). By the twenty-first century, "political action committees" manipulate politics by treating politicians as their clients and bestowing largess in return for favorable policies. Anyone who breaks rank with the patron is punished by the withdrawal of favor (i.e., political cash). For all intents and purposes, the structure of public gratitude that bedevils our society today resembles that of ancient Rome.

Although we have not seen it clearly, we are now living through a renewed conflict over gratitude and politics. The question is surprisingly stark: Will gratitude be used to undergird hierarchies of power and quid pro quo that benefit the few, or will gratefulness undo unjust practices of control to enlarge the circle of benefits for all?

The choice we make could not be more important for the future of our life together.

WOMEN TAKE ON GRATITUDE

At the end of Jane Austen's *Pride and Prejudice*, Lady Catherine de Bourgh confronts Elizabeth Bennet, the novel's heroine. Throughout the story, Lady Catherine has used her wealth to reward those who obey her and to punish those who do not, controlling the lives of all those who depend upon her patronage. Lady Catherine is also the aunt of Mr. Darcy, whom Elizabeth had once believed haughty, but whom she now loves. A rumor that Darcy and lower-status Elizabeth will soon be wed reached

Lady Catherine. Outraged that her nephew might enter into such a match, she confronts Miss Bennet to find the truth of the matter. She demands that no engagement take place.

Elizabeth will not confirm the rumor (because it is not true), but she also refuses to submit to Lady Catherine's demands: "If I am that choice, why may I not accept him?"

Lady Catherine flies into a rage, saying that such a marriage would be a "disgrace" and calling Elizabeth an "obstinate, head-strong girl" whose undesirable family connections would make a mockery of Mr. Darcy's high birth and force him from polite society. She predicts terrible consequences if Elizabeth marries Darcy, consequences that Lady Catherine herself will help bring about. She attempts to intimidate Elizabeth by pointing out her "inferior birth" and maintaining she is "of no importance in the world." Lady Catherine accuses Elizabeth of ingratitude, since she had previously welcomed the young woman to her own table: "Is there nothing due me on that score?"

Elizabeth is resolute. She will not promise to refuse an offer of marriage.

A furious Lady Catherine finishes her tirade: "You refuse, then, to oblige me. You refuse to obey the claims of duty, honor, and gratitude. You are determined to ruin him in the opinion of all his friends, and make him the contempt of the world."

Elizabeth replies: "Neither duty, nor honor, nor gratitude has any possible claim on me in the present instance." If Mr. Darcy asks, Elizabeth will say yes.

Lady Catherine cuts her off: "I take no leave of you, Miss Bennet. I send no compliments to your mother. You deserve no such attention. I am seriously displeased."[7]

Jane Austen's novels often portray conflicts between different structures of gratitude. In *Pride and Prejudice*, Lady Catherine embodies public gratitude that reflects duties of benefit and obligation, a world where gratitude is a transaction in a hierarchical society. Austen sharply criticized that form of gratitude, showing Lady Catherine as cruelly vengeful, using her status to vindictively assert her superiority. And that is the problem with gratitude and politics—the problem that eighteenth-century people experienced and tried to reform. In transactional gratitude, there are often punitive ramifications for beneficiaries, while privilege on the benefactor side continues to assert control, and neither of those things is good for society.

GRATITUDE AND THE POWER PLAY

Both the punitive and privileged aspects of gratitude are still on full display. Jane Austen's Lady Catherine de Bourgh is not just a character in a novel. Indeed, her specter haunted the 2016 American election for president in the dual ghosts of these two sides of transactional gratitude, a lens few have thought to employ in analyzing recent political events.

Gratitude as Punitive: During the Democratic primary in the spring, a story broke that Hillary Clinton had received a large fee from Goldman-Sachs for giving a speech a few years earlier. This story, in addition to news that the Clinton foundation had received cash from foreign governments, caused a firestorm. Senator Bernie Sanders demanded to see Mrs. Clinton's Goldman-Sachs speech. He wanted to know what she had said to Wall Street's wealthiest executives. He believed that the money they paid her—as well as money donated to her campaign—made her indebted to these benefactors to carry out whatever policies they wanted. "You're not going to have a government that represents all of us," Senator Sanders insisted, "so long as you have candidates like Secretary Clinton being dependent on big money interests."[8]

Dependent. Hillary Clinton was the beneficiary, not the benefactor. This meant she "owed" a debt of gratitude toward those who had given the money and was, in some way, obligated to enact policies favorable to them. Few people understood this in terms of benefactors, benefit, and beneficiary—that is, the transactional structure of gratitude. Many assumed that such big benefits come with big strings of return favors attached. In this scenario, "benefit" is nearly indistinguishable from "bribe."

With "bribe" comes payback. Certainly, no one gives a gift of hundreds of thousands of dollars without expecting something in return—or withholding future benefit if appropriate gratitude is not forthcoming. If you are on the receiving end of this transaction, you may expect the benefactor to come after you.

Essentially, Bernie Sanders wondered if Hillary Clinton would—or even could—be a free political agent. Would she be in thrall to big donors? And if she did act independently, would the donors penalize her—or the country—for not doing what they wanted?

I suspect that many people (especially given how many people eventually voted for Clinton) thought all this a ginned-up political distraction. Few, however, thought about these actions in relation to gratitude, but they really were. Although it was not presented well in the media, some people feared that benefactor, benefit, and beneficiary were locked together in a dangerous social arrangement. If anyone suggested that Clinton might actually be a benefactor (her family does run a large charitable foundation after all), such a suggestion was hard to hear. Instead, Hillary Clinton would forever be a recipient at the bottom of the gratitude cycle, always threatened by malevolent patrons, as Lady Catherine said, "a disgrace . . . the contempt of the world." Is it ever appropriate to elect a president who is a beneficiary subject to the whims of reward and revenge of unscrupulous givers? Or was this all a manufactured political attack? Perhaps. But the questions at the core of the episode are old ones indeed—questions about how gratitude, power, and obligation work in a good society.

Gratitude as Privilege: Donald Trump was born to a wealthy family, inherited a fortune, and made even more money in his own business empire. Trump depicted himself at the top of the economic pyramid, a successful self-made businessman who dispensed favors to others instead of receiving them from others. He depicted himself as the ultimate benefactor. He told this story in *The Art of the Deal,* a peculiar cross between a memoir and a self-help book. Even a quick perusal of it reveals a man who sees the world as a stage for quid pro quo. Life is a deal in which a confident "winner" gets other people to do what he wants—and makes a lot of money while doing it.

The Art of the Deal is a riff on the ancient idea of noblesse oblige, the notion that the rich are obligated by their social standing to take care of those beneath them. Noblesse oblige has, in principle, fueled much charitable giving and social good, but it is based on privilege and that the greatest benefactors come from the upper classes. Throughout the presidential campaign, Trump made claims of giving magnificent gifts to nonprofits and charities.[9] He also insisted that because he was among the world's wealthiest businessmen, he was not beholden to favors.

His wealth insulated him from paybacks to benefactors, because he did not need anything: "By self-funding my campaign, I am not controlled by my donors, special interests or lobbyists. I am only working for the people of the U.S.!"[10]

Although noblesse oblige was always a concept of privilege, it could be practiced in selfless or benevolent ways. For Trump, however, noblesse oblige is about winners and power. Privilege functions primarily as an economic and political tool, as he said in this exchange in a 2015 Republican debate:

> TRUMP: I will tell you that our system is broken. I gave to many people, before this, before two months ago, I was a businessman. I give to everybody. When they call, I give. And do you know what? When I need something from them two years later, three years later, I call them, they are there for me.
>
> UNIDENTIFIED MALE: So what did you get?
>
> TRUMP: And that's a broken system.
>
> UNIDENTIFIED MALE: What did you get from Hillary Clinton and Nancy Pelosi?
>
> TRUMP: Well, I'll tell you what, with Hillary Clinton, I said be at my wedding and she came to my wedding. You know why? She didn't have a choice because I gave.[11]

She didn't have a choice because I gave. That is the definition of transactional gratitude. Benefactors give in order to receive something in return: obedience, loyalty, or payback. This aspect of the gratitude system is about maintaining status and privilege. Gifts are about what you get in return. Beneficiaries are always in thrall to benefactors. You can either be a subject of the system, or you can control it.

No candidate ever explained this understanding of gratitude more clearly. However, Trump did not see this as negative. He had gained from the system his entire life; as he said repeatedly throughout the campaign, "Nobody knows it better than me" and "I alone can fix it." He simply wanted to be the top benefactor—one who would use the system to benefit the "right" people, those who would return him loyalty and honor. Trump believed that the system was rewarding the wrong beneficiaries. He did not want to get rid of the structure. He wanted to rebuild it. Repairing that "broken" system—shoring up the infrastructure of privileged benefits in a hierarchical system of gratitude—would make America great again.

What was really needed was to make America grateful again—with a radical restructuring of thanksgiving.

A DIFFERENT WAY?

Jane Austen excelled in depicting women as heroines standing against unjust transactional gratitude—almost as much as she loved taking down blustery benefactors. *Pride and Prejudice* is about gratitude, even about the struggle we have over gratitude in contemporary politics. *Pride and Prejudice*'s main story line— that of Elizabeth Bennet and Mr. Darcy's romance—involves gratitude. Darcy does a favor for Elizabeth's family, one that is impossible to repay. He knows that if Elizabeth learns of his magnanimity, she might feel obligated to marry him. He does not want obligatory gratitude. He wants her love freely, without indebtedness. Elizabeth does find out, and although she has fallen in love with Mr. Darcy, she fears she is now in the awkward position of beneficiary and that she cannot come to him as an equal. She rejects him. Thus, transactional gratitude actually keeps the lovers apart.

The way out of the dilemma is a different sort of gratitude, one found in humility and forgiveness. "It was gratitude," explains the narrator, "gratitude, not merely for having once loved her, but for loving her still well enough to forgive all the petulance and acrimony of her manner in rejecting him, and all the unjust accusations accompanying her rejection."[12] That alternate gratefulness—of humility and forgiveness that place all people on equal footing—opened the way of true love, and it empowered Elizabeth to stand up to Lady Catherine, the character who embodies both the privilege and punishment aspects of transactional gratitude. Elizabeth was an "ingrate" because she subverted Lady Catherine's version of gratitude. However, Elizabeth replaced it with a different vision of gratitude, one based on forgiveness and humility (as opposed to the "pride" of the punitive aspect of gratitude) and equality (as opposed to the "prejudice" of privilege). She may have been an "ingrate" in an unjust structure, but she was deeply grateful in a more just one. To Elizabeth, gratitude is not a transaction. It is the response to gifts and grace.

Elizabeth and Darcy marry, and together they create a new world at Darcy's house, Pemberley—a grand place that is both private home and public estate—through practices of humility, equality, and hospitality. At Pemberly, gratitude fosters reconciliation. By novel's end, family members, friends, and even foes (with the exception of one) are welcomed to Pemberley without threat of punishment or being subject to the demands of privilege. For two centuries, Jane Austen's charming romance has been making a stunningly radical political point: a different world of gratitude is possible. A great house is open to all—its gifts of abundance can heal and restore hope and love. Everyone is blessed. The move is from transaction to table.

And, interestingly enough, women often point the way toward that kind of grateful society. We women often find ourselves at the receiving end of corrupted forms of gratitude. So, we have learned how to come up with alternatives and create a different kind of blessed community. Pink hats and all.

8

Circles of Gratitude

The circle is a reminder that each moment is not
just the present, but is inclusive of our gratitude
to the past and our responsibility to the future.

—KAZUAKI TANAHASHI

One of the first Bible stories I remember hearing in Sunday school was the story of Zacchaeus, a short man who climbed up a tree to catch a glimpse of Jesus. It is a popular story for children, especially since it was turned into a song that captures the tale in just a few catchy lines:

Zacchaeus was a wee little man,
And a wee little man was he.
He climbed up in a sycamore tree
For the Lord he wanted to see.

And when the Savior passed that way
He looked up and said, "Zacchaeus,
You come down,
For I'm going to your house today!
For I'm going to your house today!"

If you have spent any time in church in the last forty years, chances are very good you know the Zacchaeus song. I have no idea how many times I have actually sung it or how many times I have heard it sung by a children's choir. Hand movements accompany the words—a combination that usually results in charming but hilarious performances by confused three-year-olds in tiny choir robes.

The lyrics emphasize Zacchaeus's stature, but the actual story in the Gospel of Luke emphasizes something else. Zacchaeus, a Jew, was also a chief tax collector and a very rich man. He earned that position by collaborating with Roman authorities—in effect he was a traitor to his own people. His neighbors hated him. Despite the sweet song, this is a deeply political story, one of the most trenchant social critiques of Roman quid pro quo patronage in the whole of the New Testament. Indeed, in his encounter with Zacchaeus, Jesus reveals a conflict between the Roman system of gratitude and an alternative vision of thanksgiving.

Since Zacchaeus was a Jew and not a Roman citizen, there was only one way he could become wealthy. In lands that they conquered, the Romans offered some political positions at auction to local inhabitants. The tax collectors were the main agents of the patronage system. It was a good job. While governors ensured that peace and prosperity flowed down from the emperor, tax collectors made sure that cash came up from the provinces to pay the military and enrich the noble classes in the imperial city. Tax collectors guaranteed that the empire worked and that its benefits reached those at the top.

As a subjugated person, you could essentially buy your way into higher status in the Roman system by being a tax collector, the most despised (and most necessary) of imperial middlemen. You would get rich because you were allowed to take your skim of the profit as the money headed to Rome. However, those beneath you in social standing—who paid onerous amounts of tribute monies—hated you, and those above you, who worried you might be taking more than your fair share, distrusted you. For tax collectors, wealth was as certain as unpopularity. That is how Zacchaeus got rich. Somehow, he had bought his position as a tax collector, and he had worked up from there to become chief tax collector in the important city of Jericho. Zacchaeus knew how to play the game. He was—quite literally—a climber. Success meant to gain as much status as allowed by the system and to go as high as he, a lowly Jew, could. And he had made it. He was not a "wee little man." Zacchaeus was a big man: chief tax collector of Jericho.

It should be no surprise that when Jesus, this rabbi who was healing people and stirring up crowds, came to town, Zacchaeus would want to see him and try to figure this fellow out. Was Jesus the promised Messiah who would send the Romans packing? That would have been bad for business. Maybe he worried that Jesus would inspire rebellion or encourage the masses to resist paying their taxes. Maybe Zacchaeus was just spiritually curious. Whatever the case, the crowds were huge on the day Jesus entered Jericho, and Zacchaeus (who was a short man) could not see. He needed to be aware of anything that could threaten his position. So he did what he always did—he got in front of everyone else by climbing *up* above them. This is not a charming children's story. This is a story about the guy who cuts in line, cheats on tests, and stuffs the ballot box in order to become class president. When Jesus came to town, Zacchaeus needed to keep an eye on this spiritual celebrity, and so, as the Bible says, "he ran ahead and climbed a sycamore tree to see him" (Luke 19:4). Of course he did.

When Jesus passed the tree, he looked up and saw Zacchaeus. Able to read the hearts of people, Jesus did not see a jolly fellow tangled in sycamore branches. He saw Zacchaeus, a collaborator and an agent of the Roman overlords. And what did he say? "Zacchaeus, hurry and come down!" ("Get out of that tree! Come down now!") "For I must stay at your house today." Jesus called him down, ordering him to stand as equals with him on the ground, and then invited himself to dinner.

According to Luke, Zacchaeus "hurried down and was happy to welcome him" (19:6). But the crowds watching this encounter were shocked and angry. Jesus was a lower-status person, and a good Jew. Lower-status people never invited their superiors to a meal. The whole structure of society was based upon elites doing favors for those beneath them to secure political loyalty. In normal circumstances, Zacchaeus should have invited Jesus to his home. Once Jesus accepted Zacchaeus's hospitality, then Jesus would owe Zacchaeus his gratitude, an obligation to repay the favor that had been extended to him. That, however, would have undermined Jesus's spiritual authority with the crowds who followed him. They would have wanted Jesus to reject such an overture.

But Jesus undermined this whole gratitude business by inviting himself to Zacchaeus's house. Jesus offered the gift of his presence to one who did not deserve it. This made Zacchaeus not a benefactor, but a beneficiary of a gift. Technically, Zacchaeus now owed Jesus something. Out of his sense of gratitude, Zacchaeus promised to give away half of his wealth to the poor and pay back all those whom he defrauded four times as much as he skimmed. Ultimately, it would have been impossible to give back this much money. Zacchaeus promised to bankrupt himself. In effect, he resigned his position. There is no way Zacchaeus could have remained a tax collector. He got out of the tree—extricating himself from the Roman hierarchical structure of debt and duty. In response, Jesus proclaimed: "Today salvation"—healing and wholeness—"has come to this house!" (19:9).

SETTING THE TABLE

Zacchaeus thought that gratitude was a political structure of benefactors and beneficiaries that he could manipulate for his own benefit. Then Jesus called him down from that tree and invited him to a table. "Stop climbing, Zacchaeus. Come and sit." Whereas Rome practiced gratitude as a hierarchy of political and economic obligation, of debt and duty, Jesus envisioned gratitude as hospitality of mutuality and relationship, of gift and response. Jesus opened the door for Zacchaeus to "come down" from his old life, to stop participating in a corrupt system of gratitude that oppressed his own people. In a moment, Jesus turned his world upside down: Who was the guest and who was the host? The Roman structure of gratitude collapsed when assigned roles disappeared and the conventional gifts of hospitality could not be repaid. Instead, Jesus imagined a place where oppressed and oppressor leave their "stations" and meet as friends, where forgiveness is practiced and gratitude expresses itself not in debt payment but in passing on generous gifts to others.

At the end of the story, Jesus explains that he did this because "the Son of Man came to seek out and to save the lost" (Luke 19:10). Jesus came to deliver those ensnared in the punishment and privilege of gratitude and to set them free from quid pro quo patronage. In its place, he established a table of hospitality where all are guests and no one owes anything to anyone else. Around this table, gifts pass without regard to payback or debt. Everyone sits. Everyone eats. And, recognizing that everything is a gift, all are grateful. Tree or table? Climbing to get ahead or reclining with friends? Choose. What you choose results in either slavery or abundance.

This is the ancient wisdom of gratitude, told in a Jewish political context by early Christian writers. But we can see beyond its unique religious frame to the story's larger relevance for today. Who wants to be part of a system of gratitude based on hierarchy? To be obligated to repay every favor done? Who wants to perpetuate a system that rewards privilege and is held together by indebtedness? A structure where we are pretty sure that the people above us cheated us to get there?

Think of how we depict Thanksgiving—people around a table eating a meal. In the United States, it is the romanticized image of our most primal gratitude myth: Europeans and Natives sharing around a table. Of course, it did not happen that way. But that is what myths are—stories that express something we desire, what we hope will be, and how we dream of happiness and peace. There is something in our hearts that longs to banish quid pro quo to the pages of dusty history books forever and instead create a common table where we pass gifts to one another without regard for station or status, where boundaries dissolve around plenty. That is the way of salvation. We know this, and, like Zacchaeus, many of us long for it. We just do not know how to come down from the tree.

PRO BONO AND THE GOLDEN RULE

When I started on a path to a more grateful life, I never imagined that the journey would lead to reconsidering ethics and politics, yet it seems somewhat inevitable now. Politics is about the way we structure life together. Gratitude is about mutuality, gifts, and caring, about how we give and receive, about benefactors, benefits, and beneficiaries, and about how we respond to all of that. Whether we recognize it or not, gratitude is necessary to our common life. And politics is how we organize that life. We carry around assumptions about gifts and gratitude. Those assumptions are too often invisible to us, yet they form the deep structure of our communities.

That deep structure shapes our communal choices—about the nature of gifts, about givers, and about those who receive. Gratitude and politics have always been woven together. Politics is a long history of misappropriating gratitude, about patronage, privilege, power, and quid pro quo. In the story of Jesus and Zacchaeus, Zacchaeus takes the corrupt structure for granted—the empire just is what it is. Best to go along and get along. He could not see another possibility until Jesus called him down from the tree. Jesus invited Zacchaeus to an alternative way, one that questioned Zacchaeus's assumptions and restructured his deepest sense of community.

As I thought about Jesus and Zacchaeus and ruminated on the possibility of an alternative politics of gratitude, I wondered what the opposite of quid pro quo would be. On a whim, I searched that question online—and both my question and an answer popped up written by someone on the Quora website:

> *Quid pro quo* is a Latin expression used in a legal context. It means "this for that," indicating the type of arrangement where two parties agree to make a mutual exchange. *This* is given because *that* is expected.
>
> The opposite would be *pro bono,* another Latin expression used in a legal context with contrary meaning. It means literally "for good" and perhaps is akin to "for the sake of the greater good." Something is given, and nothing is expected in return.[1]

For far too long, politics has been a game of tit for tat, a reciprocal arrangement of corrupted gratitude geared toward enriching those at the top of the social pyramid who control the flow of benefits to everyone else. Life in the Roman Empire, Jane Austen's England, and the world today; the last election, the latest headlines—all transactions of benefits and payback. The powerful act as political patrons, turning citizens into clients—if not servants or slaves—and demand gratitude and loyalty in return for goods and protection. Meanwhile, the lower ranks of the pyramid swell in numbers, and more people compete for ever more stingily dispersed services, as abundance and prosperity migrate upward to only a few. For the last two hundred years, Western democracies tried to mitigate the excesses of misused gratitude, but economic forces and the emergence of a postnational global elite overwhelmed those experiments. We are all trapped in someone else's quid pro quo game. We do not even know who is on top. Some shadow group of superrich corporate titans and economic oligarchs? At least Zacchaeus knew the boss he worked for.

Social scientists and psychologists argue that gratitude will make us happier, develop greater resiliency, and provide better outcomes of health and well-being. If gratitude is but an individualistic practice, however, it only serves to help us adjust to a fundamentally corrupted form of political life.[2] As a personal practice, gratitude helps us navigate challenges and be more content with our lives, but if we fail to understand the larger social consequences of gratitude, then it is little more. Indeed, if we still carry around inside a deep structure of gratitude as debt, obligation, and payback, it serves to reinforce hierarchical structures of injustice and spiritualizes gifts and blessings while offering only heavenly rewards to those lower down in the system.[3] Maybe Zacchaeus would have been better off keeping a gratitude journal than running after Jesus. If he had kept it private, maybe he would not have had to face the hard reality of the structures that he served.

There was, I suspect, another reason Zacchaeus kept climbing trees. He might have worked for Caesar, but he was still a Jew. He understood that God was the Creator and Giver of all gifts. He knew that his religion centered on gratitude in its great thanksgiving festivals celebrating God's abundance. He must have remembered the generosity and gratitude at the core of Jewish identity. He collaborated, yes. But it would be difficult to avoid the faith that must have tugged daily at his heart. The life of a good Jew was that of humble thanksgiving, a way that resisted the entire corrupt system of Rome. I think Zacchaeus wanted to be a good Jew. Yet in Zacchaeus's world eventually you had to choose: either you were grateful to Rome and ungrateful to God, or grateful to God and an ingrate to Rome. Accommodation was hard.

Zacchaeus knew all of this, deep inside. As a successful tax collector, he participated in a structure he thought could never change. But his heart inclined toward something else—God's dream of gifts and grace as proclaimed by the Hebrew prophets. Zacchaeus could not just be content with his personal blessings. He knew gratitude was public, communal, and political. Jesus jogged his spiritual memory, and made Zaccheaus's deep spiritual longings obvious. Jesus made him choose.

Zacchaeus had to resist the political assumptions of the world around him in favor of a different vision of the world. Often gratitude and resistance are depicted as opposing energies. It is possible to resist seeing life as a gift. It is possible to resist being thankful. We can collaborate with structures of oppression. We can be ingrates to abundance, to grace. We can continue to live in corrupt systems of payback. When our individual lives are transformed by the sort of gratefulness taught by Jesus (and other spiritual teachers), however, we begin to see that society is often toxic when it comes to gratitude. We begin to question our assumptions about the deep structure of the environment in which we find ourselves.

We might be grateful persons, with thankful hearts, and be fanatical about gratitude journals and intentions, but as soon as we walk out our front door or turn on the news, we are confronted with a world of payback, quid pro quo, corruption, and ungrateful neighbors. Thus, even for those of us who live more gratefully, our personal practices and habits are at odds with the world in which we live. We are like fish swimming in a polluted river. The chances are not very good that one healthy fish can survive in a poisoned stream. We get used to toxicity. We cannot sustain even our own health. For the good of all, we must resist the status quo, we must clean up the water. Here is where gratitude and resistance combine. Gratitude resists unhealthy environments and empowers the possibility of change. If gratitude is built upon a myth of scarcity and imperial hierarchies, it has been corrupted. If gratitude is privatized and collaborates with injustice, it is not really gratitude. Thus the better the surrounding environment, the more grateful people become, aware of gifts and abundance, open to hope, creativity, and joy. Gratitude begins with a profound awareness of abundance and builds communities of well-being and generosity. Gratitude opens toward grace.

That is what a pro bono politics could look like: renewing, reforming, and restoring our political habitat for all. Not because we expect anything in return, not out of a reciprocal obligation, but simply because it is the right thing to do and spreads benefit to the entire community. We cannot afford false forms of gratitude any longer. There appears to be some level of inchoate understanding of this right now in global politics, a deep uneasiness that the communal environment is bad for us and is working against us. Practicing pro-bono gratitude is an antidote to it all. "There is a wave of gratefulness," claims Brother David Steindl-Rast, "because people are becoming aware how important this is and how this can change our world."[4] Yet a countermovement of debt and duty is afoot as well—politics of order, resentment, and privilege are pushing the world back toward

"Rome," the long-assumed structure that uses gratitude as a tool to control.

Dismantling quid pro quo seems threatening because it is what we have known—yet many people are desperately climbing trees to get above the crowd. Setting a table of political life based around hospitality and friendship seems like kooky idealism. Even good-hearted people (as Zacchaeus surely was) imagine that it is easier to keep fixing the quid pro quo system, to make it fairer, more responsive to beneficiaries. Inside, however, we dream that one day we might be the benefactors, higher up in the system. We can throw the bums out and take our rightful place at the top of the pyramid, where we would surely make the political exchange of tit-for-tat gratitude work with liberty and justice for all. History, however, teaches us that it never happens that way.

Much contemporary political talk—from both conservatives and liberals—revolves around the notion that this structure of benefactors and benefits once worked. If only "our" people were the benefactors, we could repair the system and make it fair again. The appeal is to the past, when gratitude bound citizens together in reciprocal obligations of debt. Conservatives tend to emphasize these obligations as they affect private charity and trickle-down economics; liberals emphasize government duties like Social Security and health care (notice that we call these things "benefits" and "entitlements"—the language of gratitude is everywhere in politics). Conservatives seek to privatize the role of benefactor; liberals see the government as a benevolent provider of benefits. (Conservatives always focus on benefactors and liberals on benefits. Most politicians ignore the humanity of beneficiaries!) Both hearken back to some golden era when their particular ideal of public gratitude functioned well—whether it was the Reagan era or the Roosevelt one—and strengthened communal life, when Americans were truly grateful. Mostly, politicians say we have to return to someone's version of the old days.

That is, of course, political nostalgia. The old days never really existed as people remember, and the hierarchal structure of gratitude has never been free from graft or power grabs no matter who was in charge. The "old days" are not the answer. But a bit of ancient wisdom called the Golden Rule just might be. The biblical version is "Do to others as you would have them do to you," but the Golden Rule shows up in nearly every world religion and humanist ethical tradition in some form or other, dating back thousands of years. In addition to being called the Golden Rule, this wisdom saying is also known as the "law of reciprocity." The right kind of reciprocity. Not hierarchical, but neighborly.

That is what, at its core, gratitude is. The right kind of reciprocity, one that is not payback, one that is, instead, the sharing of gifts and care pro bono. Gratitude is an ethic of reciprocity that responds to gifts by moving them forward to others and not back "up" to benefactors. Reciprocity is necessarily communal, social, and political. Reciprocity is part of the fabric of society, but throughout history it has often oppressed, since it was based on structures of punishment and privilege. Reciprocity mutates into vengeance when linked with punishment and control; reciprocity can reinforce injustice and inequality when connected to privilege. When these forms of reciprocity are meshed with top-down structures of wealth and power, gratitude becomes (at best) noblesse oblige and (at worst) quid pro quo. This is not golden, except for those at the top.

We do need to go back—way back. To the wisdom of the Golden Rule. "Do to others" lays out a vision of benevolent responsiveness, a kind of reciprocity between people that levels the field of relationships and benefits and provides a moral template for gratitude in public life. First of all, the rule has no hierarchical structure. No one is on top, no person is identified as wealthier or smarter, and there is no particular class of benefactors. There are only "others" and you. This is an equal-footing rule! Second, the Golden Rule reminds us that all human beings share in suffering and want. Sooner or later, everyone will be on the receiving end because of need. You may be the benefactor now, but at some point you will need the help and goodwill of others. You will be a beneficiary. The truth of the matter is you are both benefactor and beneficiary all the time. The Golden Rule equalizes and humanizes. It is a rule, as in *regula*, "a rhythm or pattern" of life, for our common existence.

The Golden Rule is a concise summary of Jesus's encounter with Zacchaeus. "Come down from that tree," Jesus insisted, "and sit at a table where all people are hosts and guests, givers and receivers together." Indeed, Jesus ties the Golden Rule to a litany of abundance: "Do not worry about your life. . . . Strive first for the kingdom of God . . . and all these things will be given to you as well"; "Ask and it will be given you; search, and you will find"; "How much more will your Father in heaven give good things to those who ask him" (Matt. 6:25–7:11). Jesus promises that gifts, like wildflowers in a field, surround our lives as extravagant goodness and care. There is enough, enough for all people, in all times, and in all places. In the biblical view, God gives all gifts, and we human beings accept them and pass them on to one another. We never owned them to begin with. We are only mediators and stewards, not benefactors in our own right. Because the source of gifts is the Creator and creation, benefit extends beyond any one community, tribe, or political arrangement to the whole human race. Every person, no matter how rich or poor, how powerful or powerless, is first of all a receiver of this radical abundance.[5]

Therefore, Jesus exclaims, "In everything do to others as you would have them do to you; for this is the law and the prophets" (Matt. 7:12). This directive is not solely about personal or private ethics. This principle encompasses humanity—how we treat everybody. Jesus states that the Golden Rule is the *law*— the rule that governs the whole community of God's people— and the *prophets*—the divine imperative for compassion and empathy for all creation. "Do unto others" is a communal command and a cosmic intention, a structure for political life here and now as well as the hope for the future. This is a circle of gift and response. Of this structure, Peter Leithart says, "Gifts flow on and on. . . . The circle is infinite because God is the source of *every* gift, even gifts mediated through human beings."[6]

All gifts exist before we give them. God gives gifts. Creation gives gifts. We receive and we pass on. "Love your neighbor as yourself." There is work for us to do, but it is good work. When we take on the work of the Golden Rule, when our gratitude flows from this, we can cleanse the toxic environment around us. We can work for the good of all—the politics of gratitude.

A DEBT-FREE WORLD

If gifts precede benefactors, there is no expectation to return the favor (because givers are simply passing on a gift, and other gifts will come their way). Receivers are freed from the "debts" of gratitude and may graciously pass whatever gifts they can on to others instead of paying back a benefactor. Jesus taught this clearly: "If you lend to those from whom you hope to receive, what credit is that to you? Even sinners lend to sinners, to receive as much again. But love your enemies, do good, and lend, expecting nothing in return" (Luke 6:34–35). The free movement of gifts—in a nonhierarchical way—is the very heart of Christianity. According to Leithart, givers impose no debt, and the only debt of receivers is to love others. He refers to this as an "infinite circle" of gratitude and contrasts it to the closed system of obligation that bound people into oppressive forms of patronage and payback. Gratitude is not about manners and courtesy. It is never truly private. It is about the nature of society. It is deeply and profoundly political and opens us to the revolutionary idea of a debt-free community that shares in the mutual benefit of creation's gifts while unmasking privilege and permanently undoing all forms of slavery.[7] We must move away from debt-and-duty constructs toward a vision of gratitude as gift and response.

If that sounds too political—a discussion with little place in a book on either gratitude or spirituality—consider, for a moment, that this idea appears in one of the most significant of all of the New Testament's teachings: the Lord's Prayer.

I grew up in a Methodist church. Every Sunday, we recited the prayer that Jesus shared with his disciples:

> Our Father who art in heaven,
> Hallowed be thy name.
> Thy kingdom come,

Thy will be done,
On earth as it is in heaven.
Give us this day our daily bread;
And forgive us our trespasses,
As we forgive those who trespass against us;
And lead us not into temptation,
But deliver us from evil.

As a child, I liked those comforting words, especially that mysterious-sounding one, "trespasses." I had no idea what a trespass was, but it seemed important that Jesus would insist that they be forgiven, whether we did them or if someone did them to us. It would not be until I was thirteen, in Confirmation class, that a Methodist pastor finally told me that a "trespass" was a poetic word for "sin." The Lord's Prayer asks that our sins be forgiven and that we might forgive anyone who sinned against us. Aha! That made sense!

A decade or so later, I visited a Presbyterian church for the first time. The Lord's Prayer was included in the service. I mouthed the familiar words, "Give us this day our daily bread; and forgive us our . . ." I almost said "trespasses," but the bulletin said, "Forgive us our debts as we forgive our debtors." What? Debts? The Lord's Prayer is about money? This made absolutely no sense to me, and I missed those lyrical "trespasses."

Trespasses or debts? What was going on here? The New Testament is written in Greek. *Hamartia* is the Greek word for "sin"; it means "to miss the mark," "to err," or "to be fatally flawed." That is how we usually think about sin; it is about failing to make good choices or doing something naughty, perhaps because of some sort of deep character flaw. But Jesus didn't speak Greek. Jesus spoke Aramaic, a local language in the ancient Middle East related to Hebrew.

The word I had learned as "trespasses" was most likely the Aramaic word *choba*. And it is the translation of that word that is the source of an important distinction. There are two versions of the Lord's Prayer in the New Testament, one in the Gospel of Luke (11:2–4), the other in the Gospel of Matthew (6:9–13). Luke's version of the Lord's Prayer uses *hamartia* to translate *choba*, but Matthew's version does not. Matthew chooses a different word, *opheilemata*, which means "debts." He does so for a very particular reason. Most rabbis in Jesus's time—and Jesus was a rabbi—understood sin as "debt," with the connotation of weight, burdens, and obligations. Jewish theology taught that human beings "owe" only one debt (and it is not a "burden" but a joy): we owe God faithfulness and praise because God alone is the giver of all gifts (the "daily bread" of the prayer). False debts enslave us to idols, for there is no Giver but God.

In Matthew's Gospel, the Lord's Prayer immediately follows the Beatitudes. Jesus's sermon proclaims blessing upon outcasts and the oppressed and then moves to freedom from debt. The prayer literally reads, "Forsake our debts, as we forsake our debtors." These are cancelled debts. Jesus teaches his followers to leave behind the whole system of indebtedness that obligates people to Caesar. Essentially, the Lord's Prayer is a takedown of Roman economics and politics. The prayer describes an economy of abundance that begins in heaven, where there is always enough, where all are blessed. Heaven is a vision of what this world is to be, a community that trusts God's provision and holds no one in debt. "Sin" is when the circle of abundance is abused—and when we see "gifts" as something we have earned, own, and can make others earn—and we set up a system of indebtedness whereby we enrich ourselves and control others. In the Bible, sin is debt, and debt is sin.

The Lord's Prayer *is* comforting. We can live free from the naughty things we do or the naughty things done to us. But it is not only about some spiritualized idea of sin, about our flaws and misdeeds. This radical prayer undermines imperial economics. The entire ancient Roman world was structured on debt, a political system in which debts were discharged by tributes, loyalty, and utter obedience to Caesar. The whole world was indebted to Caesar, and the whole earth was his by right. Everyone and everything owed him. Jesus says no. He prays: "Free us from debt, from holding others in debt, and from our anger against those who hold us in debt. Release us from the entanglements of debt slavery. Free us from Caesar's yoke. We long to live only in gratitude to God." At the heart of Jesus's prayer is politics.

In the prayer, Jesus restates one of the most ignored directives of the Hebrew Bible: "Every seventh year you shall grant a remission of debts. . . . Every creditor shall remit the claim that is held against a neighbor, not exacting it of a neighbor who is a member of the community, because the LORD's remission has been proclaimed" (Deut. 15:1–2). Every seven years, all debts were to be cancelled.[8] All debts. And to really whoop it up, every forty-nine years, all land was to be returned to its original owners. No one was to work the land for an entire year; people were to simply live from the land's natural abundance (Lev. 25: 8–13). The Bible calls us to Sabbath and depicts a world without work, a world free of debt. Imagine how grateful we would be—a jubilee of gratitude.

TABLE GRACE

I once was scolded for arranging the desks in my classroom in circles rather than rows. The dean worried that seating students in the round violated "the good order of the classroom." Although rearranging desks in circles might seem a pretty small matter, it really is not. Over the years, other teachers and professors have told me that they have had similar run-ins with authorities. Friends in business have shared stories of switching out rectangular meeting tables for round ones and encountering intense opposition to the change. And woe betide any member of the clergy who dares suggest taking out rows of pews and replacing them with church-in-the-round. Congregations have fired ministers for far less. Circles can be upsetting. We like our rows—clear lines, leaders up front. Anything else gets messy.

The social structures we inherit are often invisible to us. For many generations, the structure of Western culture imprinted on our imaginations was that of rows, lines, and pyramids. We were taught that everything was ordered from top to bottom, in vertical structures of family, social institutions, and politics by role, gender, and race.

Yet there have always been those who questioned this structure. In the United States, people from the margins or the bottom—mostly women, Native peoples, and African Americans—criticized and challenged these assumptions and arrangements. They envisioned and practiced different structures of social relations, typically based in greater mutuality, shared resources, and an appreciation of diversity. And they generally talked about circles instead of pyramids and lines. Although gratitude has not often been an explicit part of the argument for an alternative structure, it is striking how often themes of abundance, thankfulness, and the Golden Rule recur in these visions. Among African Americans, the circle is an apt description of the beloved community. Feminist writers regularly employ metaphors of tables where ethics center on "care" as the primary moral quality. Native Americans call tribal councils in circles, often building in the round. In all three, gratitude is not deployed hierarchically, but it is a response to gifts and giving that binds people in emotionally meaningful and socially equal ways.

Sometime along the way, I stopped thinking about how to "fit" in an angular structure and started thinking about setting the table of my life, and that meant reenvisioning how I saw the world. Instead of verticality, with God or some authority on top, the world emerged as concentric circles of community. The picture looked like this:

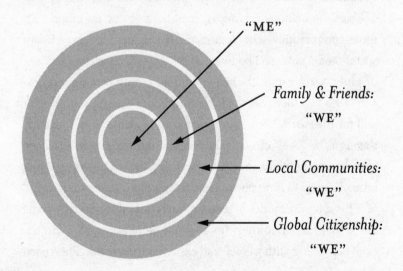

"ME"

Family & Friends:
"WE"

Local Communities:
"WE"

Global Citizenship:
"WE"

At the center of the circle is "me." I am certain some will say that this is the problem of the modern world: self-centeredness. In some contexts, they may be right, but here I am referring to the necessary positive aspects of personal development. Self-awareness, personal experience, seeing the world with our own eyes, and a keen embrace of our unique identity—being who we really are—form the basis for friendship, love, commitment, mature faith, wisdom, and even community. To know oneself is an ancient mandate, something practiced and proclaimed by history's greatest spiritual leaders and philosophers. Those who do not operate from a base of realistic self-knowledge often experience great difficulty in personal relationships and in community life.

From that central "me," our lives unfold in concentric circles of community, each circle creating a larger "we." The most intimate "we" is that of family and close friends. The expanded "we" of neighbors consists of those in close proximity to us, people in common causes or with whom we share interests (like sports, hobbies, or volunteer groups), members of our faith and religious communities, schoolmates and colleagues, and those in our social media circles. The final—and widest—circle is the "we" of global citizenship, the whole human family in a shared destiny, who together bear the responsibility to care for one another and for the earth. We begin with a healthy sense of self, expand through the "we" circles, and eventually experience the deep interdependent life of "me" and "we" flourishing together. Being human means finding oneself in these circles of community.

This circular model is true for each one of us. In the single circle that makes up the whole world, there are myriad circles, each beginning with a "me" and expanding outward. The vision is that of throwing a thousand pebbles into a pool; as each pebble splashes the surface and ripples outward, the concentric waves of single stones collide and intersect with the swells created by all the others. It may seem chaotic, but there is pattern, movement, and relationship to it all, this world of human circles.

The circle is one of the oldest ways of understanding the deep structure of human community. The pond, with its ever-widening waves, is an ancient metaphor for both spirituality and ethics. Through the centuries, different cultures employed other circular images to frame their political and social lives: the kiva, the dance, the campfire, the round table. Some of humankind's wisest and most beautiful dreams of creation, love, and justice are those of expanding circles.

Not pyramids, not hierarchies. People at the top, or people who want to be at the top, of such structures might dream of them. The rest of us? Who really wants to live in a pyramid-shaped world? Pyramids have been humanity's nightmare. Whenever we long for hierarchy, we are longing for order in what we think to be chaos. We build temples and towers to reach the gods: we plead for a warrior chief or king to save us; we make icons and idols of those we aspire to be. But such schemes for fixing things always fail. Always. Our pyramids wind up benefiting only the few, while most of us stand at the base begging for favors or dreaming of our own ascent to the crown, or capstone, or penthouse.

Even gratitude got caught up in the structure of pyramids, becoming a tool of privilege, payback, and control. The most tender and most moving of human emotions, the deepest ethic of sharing and mutual care, was perverted into a mechanism of debt and duty by systems doomed to fail.

It is time to say no more. It is time to reclaim gratefulness. In our hearts, we do not really want pyramids. We long to live in an infinite circle of gift and response. Abundance, receiving gifts, passing benefit to all: this is the nature of things. It is the sort of gratitude that resists injustice. Gratitude is what Moses taught, what the prophets proclaimed, what Jesus practiced, what enlightened the Buddha, what Native elders and medieval saints knew, what meditation reveals, what human arts and sciences point toward, and what, if you are anything like me, you dream of. A pro bono world, all invited to the table to feast. Gratitude is right here, right now. The world will change when we know gratitude for what it is, when it is rightly experienced as both the center and circumference of the circle.

AT THE WOMEN'S March, I waited a long while from the time I arrived until my friends finally found me on those rocks. For well over an hour, I had nothing to do but sit on the rocks and wait.

Another group gathered nearby. They had arrived even earlier than I had—twenty or thirty Native Americans, mostly women in traditional dress, Sioux from Standing Rock. "Water Is Sacred," "NO DAPL," "Protect Mother Earth!" and "Water IS Life" read their signs. Their prayers began with chanting; then they added drumming. The prayers grew stronger and louder; the haunting sounds of supplication echoed across the museum's patio. The women smudged, lifting their bowls of smoky incense toward the sky and waving feathers to wash the smoke over the crowd. Theirs was a liturgy of protest, and the prayers seemed to arise from the earth itself to cry out for justice and peace. As the scent of sage surrounded me, I joined their chant with my own silent prayer: "God, who breathed over the waters and created all that is, save us, strengthen us; may we awaken to the sacred everywhere."

The drumbeat quickened, and the women formed a circle and started to dance. The patio had become very crowded, but people pushed back to make way for the ring as it pulsated with holy supplications. Many of us watched transfixed.

Then a Sioux woman grabbed the hand of a white woman standing nearby. "Dance," she insisted. "Join the dance!" Other dancers took the hands of other women: "Dance with us!" The circle widened, bringing in more dancers whose skin tones reflected every shade from black to white. People laughed and chanted and circled around, holding hands, praying for the world, for the nation, for our souls.

In my mind, the Native rhythms melded into the refrain of an old Gospel hymn, a song I had known since childhood: "May the circle be unbroken, by and by, Lord, by and by." That song is about a holy circle, one that exists only in heaven after we die. We sang it a lot when I was small. But, here, on the patio of the National Museum of the American Indian in Washington, D.C., as a protest against a new president was about to begin, the circle existed. Right in front of me.

This circle, this dance, had existed since the beginning of time, a circle where all joined together with the song of the universe. It was deeply spiritual. It was profoundly political. The gift of the dance had been given long ago—and the dancers participated in it and passed it on to others. No hierarchy, no quid pro quo. The whole world is grace: gifts received, gifts given. The circle widened, inviting all nearby to join. It kept expanding, bringing people in; more room was made for the dance. An infinite circle.

All this had unfolded around me, unexpected and unplanned. I felt so grateful. I felt empowered to love and do justice, to do better and practice a life of gratitude. In a time of fear and despair, people were dancing in the streets. The politics of patronage and pyramids, an ancient system of corrupted gratitude, seemed to have won the day over there in the White House. But here, in its shadow, we created a circle of abundance, justice, prayer, and hope. It was gratitude, and it was protest.

The dancers came nearer where I sat on the rocks. A woman, her dark hair braided, her eyes blazing with joy, reached toward me. Her hand out, she said, "Come down. Join in."

I stared at the inviting hand, unable to move. Thankfulness filled my heart. Even though my friends had not arrived, I was not alone. The circle had found me.

I felt grateful. We would be grateful in the face of injustice. And I knew that gratitude could change everything.

A Call to the Grateful Way

Gratitude is the wine of the soul. Go on. Get drunk!

—ATTRIBUTED TO RUMI

I started this book in the spring of 2016. Thus, as one of the most conflicted years in American political history unfolded, I was researching happiness and reading books on positive psychology, histories of gratitude, articles on gratitude and social ethics, medical papers on gratitude and health outcomes, and spiritual memoirs of thanksgiving. Rarely have I felt more out of sync with the world around me. While anger and division mounted, I buried myself in gratefulness. Everything I read said the same thing: fear and anger are dangerous to our souls, and gratitude is good for us. Each day, however, the news re-

vealed how we had lost much of our collective sense of gratitude for each other, the gifts of life, and the beauty of the world.
The gratitude gap was not only some lack of manners on my
part, some personal flaw of mine for failing to say thank you.
Ingratitude—the sort that grows from entitlement, anxiety, and
fear—appeared to be one source of our political problems, like
an emotional toxin released into the headwaters of a river.

It was difficult to write about thanksgiving through spring
and summer of 2016. I decided to wait for the elections to pass
to tackle the hard work of writing, hoping a calmer mood might
arise when "thank you" could come more naturally.

That moment never arrived.

Facing a deadline, I had to work. So I came to write a gratitude book during the first one hundred days of the Trump presidency. The news turned into a constant litany of chaos. Family
members became unable to talk to each other. Friendships were
broken over politics. Social media became the front line in a vir-
tual civil war, with nastiness and shame its primary weapons,
and everyone was conscripted, willingly or not. Anger did not
abate. It got worse. Every. Single. Day.

During those same weeks, I struggled with a number of
health issues, my husband went through significant changes
with his work, and we experienced an unexpected family crisis. This series of external and internal emotional shocks undermined any sense of stability that I had previously trusted. Most
days I did not want to get out of bed.

A friend asked me, "What are you working on?"

"A book about gratitude," I ventured.

She stared at me, eyes wide with disbelief. "You have got to
be kidding. How is that going?"

"I'm not kidding," I replied, answering the first question. And to the second: "It is going slowly. Very slowly."

She laughed. "Good luck with that." Then she added more seriously, "I don't feel grateful. I know you don't."

She was right. Every day I faced the daunting task of writing about gratitude when I felt none. I remembered how optimistically I had imagined this book in the months before the election. I had vowed to keep a journal, practice yoga, write gratitude letters, and become more disciplined than I have ever been. I hoped that pursuing gratefulness would make me healthier and happier. I was chasing after the "secret that would change everything." After all, that is what the gratitude books I read promised.

Instead of embracing my perfect life of gratitude, however, I found myself rereading the book of Job, the Bible's grimmest account of anger and loss:

> Do not human beings have a hard service on earth,
> and are not their days like the days of a
> laborer? . . .
> I am allotted months of emptiness,
> and nights of misery are apportioned to me.
> When I lie down I say, "When shall I rise?"
> But the night is long,
> and I am full of tossing until dawn.

JOB 7:1, 3—4

I had not quite sunk to Job's level of suffering, but I could relate. There were plenty of reasons not to feel thankful. There are always reasons not to be thankful.

Even though I have struggled with gratitude my whole life, very little prepared me the emotional shock that twisted my heart into knots after November 2016. I struggled with prayer and meditation. Going to church brought scant comfort, mostly emptiness and sometimes pain. I had to remind myself to breathe. On my desk sat the project—that book on gratitude. I did not want to think about gratefulness. But I had to. I knew that I could never write well unless—*somehow*—I found my way to thanks. Oddly enough, I was being held accountable for gratitude by a book that did not exist.

So I did the only thing I could think of doing—simply saying "thanks" as I went through the day. I woke up with a brief prayer: "Thank you that I am alive." I got coffee and breakfast: "Thank you for this food, this day." I looked out the window: "Thank you for sunshine." I went into my office: "Thank you for words, for work." I noticed how I was feeling: "Thank you that my fever isn't 103 today." I thought of my family: "Thank you that we have each other." I watched the news: "Thank you that no one blew up the world today."

Even when it comes to thankfulness, sometimes you have to take what you can get. I took nothing for granted.

So while the rest of the world analyzed and dissected the first one hundred days of Trump, I practiced one hundred days of gratitude. Maybe it should be called one hundred days of tentative gratitude. It was the best I could do, these arrows of appreciation aimed at God or the universe or whoever would listen. Over the weeks, with my hapless prayers, I discovered something quite unexpected: gratitude, like interest, compounds. This simple form of giving thanks made me pay attention and start looking for particular reasons to be grateful. There would always be grounds for ingratitude. Always. Seeking out the small things for which I could give thanks, however, changed my field of spiritual and emotional vision. I learned not to focus on what was lacking. The words of the Buddha, a prayer I had begun to say most days, began to make sense:

> Let us rise up and be thankful,
> For if we didn't learn a lot today,
> At least we learned a little,
> And if we didn't learn a little,
> At least we didn't get sick,
> And if we got sick,
> At least we didn't die;
> So, let us all be thankful.[1]

Slowly I began to feel more resilient and rested easier at night. Gratitude is not a form of passive acceptance or complicity. Rather, it is the capacity to stare doubt, loss, chaos, and despair right in the eye and say, "I am still here." It is like the mantra of British theoretical physicist Stephen Hawking: "While there's life, there is hope." Being alive is radical gratitude.

Gratitude is defiance of sorts, the defiance of kindness in the face of anger, of connection in the face of division, and of hope in the face of fear. Gratefulness does not acquiesce to evil—it resists evil. That resistance is not that of force or direct confrontation. Gratitude undoes evil by tunneling under its foundations of anger, resentment, and greed. Thus, gratitude strengthens our character and moral resolve, giving each of us the possibility of living peaceably and justly. It untwists knotted hearts, waking us to a new sense of who we are as individuals and in community. Being thankful is the very essence of what it means to be alive, and to know that life abundantly.

Gratitude is not a psychological or political panacea, like a secular prosperity gospel, one that denies pain or overlooks injustice, because being grateful does not "fix" anything. Pain, suffering, and injustice—these things are all real. They do not go away. Gratitude, however, invalidates the false narrative that these things are the sum total of human existence, that despair is the last word. Gratitude gives us a new story. It opens our eyes to see that every life is, in unique and dignified ways, graced: the lives of the poor, the castoffs, the sick, the jailed, the exiles, the abused, the forgotten as well as those in more comfortable physical circumstances. Your life. My life. We all share in the ultimate gift—life itself. Together. Right now.

Gratitude evens the score, none are better than others; instead, we are all beneficiaries and, in turn, we are all benefactors to each other. The first act of being human is receiving the gift of breath, and as we go through life we continually receive. We sit at a table of gifts; we pass gifts on to others. Those gifts should not indenture others to "our" largess, for ultimately we own nothing. Death reminds us of that. But to pass on gifts, to live gratefully, is to liberate ourselves and humanity from the slavery of payback and debt, of entitlement, privilege, and superiority.

Gratitude calls us to sit together, to imagine the world as a table of hospitality. To feed one another. To feast, to dance in the streets. To know and celebrate abundance.

Gifts and gratefulness.

Gratitude empowers us. It makes joy and love possible. It re-arranges the way we see and experience what is all around us. Gratitude makes all things new. It transforms how we understand what is broken and gives us the ability to act more joyfully and with hope. That is why gratitude is central to all the world's religions. As a practice, it embodies the wisdom of humanity's greatest spiritual teachers: the love of neighbor. Gratitude takes us from abstract belief to living compassion in the world. Gratitude is strongest, clearest, most robust, and radical when things are really hard. Really hard. All-is-lost hard.

MY HUSBAND GAVE me a purple baseball cap inscribed with the words "Make America Grateful Again."

"Thanks. Nice hat," I said to him. "But how do we do it?" Slogans are fine. Actions are better.

There are two levels to practicing gratitude: the personal and the public. We need both to move ahead.

Personal Practice: In many ways, personal practice is easier and a good place to begin. I actually carry around a tiny paperback in my purse, *The Little Book of Gratitude* by Robert Emmons, as a physical reminder to engage at least one practice of thanks each day. In it, he lays out what he calls an "ARC" model of gratitude:

> Gratitude
> *amplifies* goodness,
> *rescues* us from negative emotions, and
> *connects* us to others in meaningful ways.[2]

Amplify, Rescue, Connect: the "ARC" of the grateful way. In all of his books, however, Dr. Emmons recognizes the realistic struggle toward grateful living: "Although . . . cultivating gratitude in our life and in our attitude to life allows us to flourish, it can be difficult to accomplish."[3] As you seek to live ARC, remember that Noah's "ark" was difficult to build and that Martin Luther King's "arc" of justice is long. Make it part of your practice to acknowledge that gratitude is not easy.

One of the most helpful guides to cultivating gratitude comes from Mary Jo Leddy. Among the many books on gratitude, her *Radical Gratitude* goes far beyond health-and-happiness approaches to gratitude and instead emphasizes gratitude as personal and political liberation. Over the months of this project, Leddy's words sustained me and fired my spiritual imagination. She insists that gratitude is a transformation—and the path toward a life-giving society.

To get there, she proposes ten "habits of being that can help us live with spirit . . . in a dispirited time and place." I quote her list here in its entirety, because I could not come up with a better one! Those habits include:

1. *Begin* before *you are ready.* "Beginning steps in gratitude do not have to be great or grand. They need only be real."
2. *Practice gratitude in prayers,* reflections, chants, and meditations.
3. *Gather with "like-spirited" people.* Find or start a group committed to practicing gratefulness as a way of life.
4. *Live more simply.* Let go of material things that burden you.
5. *Look for good examples of grateful people* in your life and from history. Learn from them.
6. *Think with your heart.* Trust your feelings of gratefulness and your longings for a better way of life.

7. *See differently.* Develop "soft eyes."
8. *Be connected to a longer wisdom tradition,* one that helps you understand the spiritual insights of the past.
9. *Find a beloved community,* a neighborhood or worship gathering, and be part of it, really part of it.
10. *"Contemplate the face of the world."* Gratitude empowers us to stare at reality and overcome what is challenging, violent, and evil.[4] Do not turn away from the world, turn toward it.

Do not feel you need to do all ten things. Start with whatever inspires you and move toward what calls you. Trust your unique path.

Public Practice: Leddy's list is a hinge between personal and public practices of gratitude, but if we want to create a politics of gratitude, we need to develop specific practices for shaping our common life. If it is difficult to live gratefully as individuals, achieving a communal sense of gratitude will challenge us in profound ways. There is little guidance on the topic regarding specific public practices, but there are general principles that open our imaginations to the possibilities ahead. For example, these words from a young Catholic ethicist caught my attention, as he explains the Golden Rule, abundance, and gifts:

> The politics of gratitude necessarily leads to a focus on the common good and a *whole life* commitment to securing conditions that reflect the worth and dignity of all. It leads one to affirm the universal destination of goods—the recognition that the goods of creation "are destined for the whole human race." One's claim

to such goods, to one's most basic needs, is just as legitimate if one is an orphan in the Democratic Republic of the Congo as if one is born to a Senator or CEO in one of the wealthy enclaves of the United States.[5]

The core concern—*the goods of creation are destined for the whole human race*—is a powerful political description of gift-and-response gratitude. How might we achieve this together? Two things seem key in moving forward: practicing gratitude in community and learning a new language of public gratitude.

First, communities should focus on gratitude. Businesses, schools, universities, denominations, civic groups, and even small towns could designate a "year of gratitude." I know a few clergy who have done this in congregations and, to a person, each has told me that cultivating gratitude changed their church. Indeed, one woman said, "We went from practicing complaint to practicing thanks. It remade us."

But what if it was not just a single congregation? What if an entire denomination took a year to practice gratitude? What if every school-board meeting started with a few minutes of gratitude? What if colleges and universities included "appreciations" along with evaluations? What if businesses emphasized how grateful they were for their workers and customers? We cannot create a politics of gratitude if we fail to practice together, and smaller-scale organizations like churches and denominations, schools and colleges, and businesses and town councils are the logical places to begin.

But communal gratitude cannot—and should not—be compulsory. Forcing gratitude, especially when required by those in positions of power, is another way of placating authoritar-ian egos or asserting control in hierarchical systems. Required gratefulness only fosters resentment. Communities could, how-ever, design their own gratitude covenants whereby participants freely consent to mutual expressions and practices of apprecia-tion in family life, learning, work, and governing. "Covenant," derived from Latin for "come together, unite, and agree," has often been used in restrictive and exclusionary ways. What if organizations, institutions, and communities came together in circles of thanks? Not just as a one-day holiday of celebration, but in the form of stated public commitments to the sharing of gifts for the common good?

Second, we need to frame a new political language. As pointed out in earlier chapters, much of our current political language echoes the language of debt-and-duty gratitude. We need to shift toward a political language of gift and response. We should rethink the whole language of social programs, for instance. "Entitlement" is the very antithesis of gratitude, and it provokes sharp, competitive feelings between citizens. Far better is a language of "benefit." We—all of us—can, should, and do benefit from the goods of public resources and economic growth (like education, transportation, and clean air and wa-ter). We need to recognize that our lives are profoundly depen-dent upon goods and gifts that others created and, in some way, shared. We all receive, and we all give. No one is only a "taker" or a "maker."

The role of government is not as "benefactor"; rather, demo-cratic government can be understood as a process to fairly dis-tribute social benefit, to equalize "tailwinds" for all citizens so they can achieve full, safe, and meaningful lives. Corporations

cannot be benefactors either, but they could be compelled to expand the circle of economic benefit wider—as well as to steward
natural resources to benefit humanity and our environmental future. Governments and businesses need to be rightly understood
as institutions that are receivers of gifts as well—and they too
are responsible to pay forward what they have received.

We desperately need to banish quid pro quo from our communal life altogether and replace it with pro bono thinking. If
we start to reimagine our politics as being about stewardship,
abundance, and care, we move naturally toward practicing gratitude in community. I do not know about you, but I would love
to hear politicians, civic leaders, businesspeople, teachers, and
clergy speaking of a future where gift-and-response gratitude
frames our public life. The words we use, the speeches we cheer,
and the stories we tell can lead us in new directions in community, in our politics, and across the globe.

Lists are not meant to condemn you or make you feel guilty.
Think of these general lists—Emmons's program, Leddy's ten
habits, or my suggestions for a new politics—as frameworks
for building gratitude in your life and communities. Work on
pieces of them in their own time; there is no requirement to do
everything at once. Borrow freely from different lists, for none
of them exclude the others, as they often overlap in the wisdom
offered. Keep in mind the framework presented in this book:
gratitude is for "me" and "we"; it includes both emotions and
ethics; and it has a deep structure—its truest shape is that of a
round table. *Me, we, feelings, actions, circle.* Attend to those five
things: your feelings and actions, your participation in communal feelings and actions, and how you experience and help create
that infinite circle of gratitude.

Practicing gratitude calls us to better lives, and a better world. And begin *before* you are ready. Even when a million reasons to not feel grateful stand in your way. That is when gratitude is at its best. It took me one hundred days to understand this. My husband observed, "You know, gratitude saved your life in the midst of all the chaos." He was right. Gratitude became both my refuge and my rallying cry. It made a huge difference. Trust me.

A CENTURY AGO, Albert Schweitzer, theologian and Nobel Peace Prize winner, remarked:

> The greatest thing is to give thanks for everything.
> He who has learned this knows what it means to live.
> He has penetrated the whole mystery of life: giving
> thanks for everything.[6]

He was right: to learn gratitude is to know the "mystery" of life. But he was also wrong in a very important way.

Every day there are reasons not to feel grateful and not to practice gratitude. Terrible, distressing, painful, and awful things happen all the time. The emotions of thanks elude us, and it is easy to choose ingratitude. Yet when I watch the news and fear grips my heart about whatever comes next, when a friend is diagnosed with cancer, or when a loved one dies, that Bible verse, the one Albert Schweitzer alluded to, the one I memorized as a teenager, calls toward a better way: "In everything give thanks." It does not say, as Schweitzer seems to have misquoted, "*For* everything give thanks." Gratitude never calls us to give thanks *for* anything that is evil or unjust, never *for* violence, lying, oppression, or suffering. Do not be grateful *for* these things.

The Greek word is *en*, which means "in, with, within, throughout." It locates us here and now, in the past, and in the future; in happiness, in despair; in all things, in all times, in all situations. Gratefulness grounds our lives in the world and with others, always locating the gifts and grace that accompany our way. Gratitude is an emotion. Gratitude is an ethical way of life. It is a disposition, an awareness, a set of habits. But ultimately, gratitude is a place—perhaps *the* place—where we find our truest and best selves.

To know the mystery of life is to be grateful in all things. *In* all things, *with* all things, *through* all things.

I have discovered that I am no longer an ingrate, but I am living *in* gratitude. Sometimes the world turns on a preposition. To be grateful *in* these days is an act of resistance, of resilience, of renewal. My journey started because I did not know how to write thank-you notes. And it led me to understand that a politics of gratitude is a way of healing and compassion—perhaps even salvation. I invite you to the journey from ingratitude to gratefulness and to find yourself part of a like-spirited community. You are not alone. There are many on the road.

Give thanks.

Live in gratitude.

There is a place for you at the table.

THANK YOU

As I write these words, the last leaves are falling from the trees and Thanksgiving is a week away. It seems so appropriate. To acknowledge those who contributed to this project is another way of giving thanks for the community of friends, writers, scholars, colleagues, and makers and lovers of books who constantly give gifts of their support, insights, expertise, and artistry to me and to the larger world.

This project took me into the fields of ethics and psychology, areas that have long intrigued me but are not native to me. I am particularly grateful to Dr. Robert Emmons, who patiently responded to my e-mail queries, Mary C. Ray, LCSW, who has long insisted to me that gratitude is central to health and spiritual well-being, and Dr. Joseph Stewart-Sicking, whose depth of knowledge in psychology and theology is second to none. These professionals are not responsible for any mistakes that I may have made in trying to interpret and explain the importance of research in their fields.

Some of the most life-giving and provocative ideas in this book were birthed while I served as a spiritual companion to

Valley Presbyterian Church in Portola Valley, California, for a couple weeks in October 2016. That congregation inspired a sermon on Zacchaeus that changed my entire understanding of the political dimensions of the New Testament. I feel they gave me far more than I gave them, and I am profoundly grateful for their hospitality.

Several close friends listened as I made my way through the struggle that accompanied writing this book—notably Marianne Borg, Julie Ingersoll, and Teresa Sherrill. Colleagues Brian McLaren and John Philip Newell added insightful perspectives just when I needed them. I am lucky to have a trusted group of interlocutors and spiritual guides through social media—a diverse set of folks including clergy, journalists, and authors—who actually encourage me, hold me accountable, and keep me sane. Some of their comments and experiences show up in this narrative, as well as their gentle corrections and bibliographic knowledge. Two authors I have never met—Br. David Steindl-Rast and Mary Jo Leddy—transformed my spiritual imagination through their amazing books on gratitude.

Nothing in my life would be as it is without the long professional and personal relationship I have with HarperOne. The words "thank you" seem woefully inadequate to express what I feel to Mark Tauber, Laina Adler, Mickey Maudlin, Suzanne Wickham, Katy Hamilton, Ann Edwards, Anna Paustenbach, Lisa Zuniga, and Harper's legion of artists, book designers, and copyeditors. I hope, that after reading *Grateful*, they know I really mean it. And I am deeply appreciative that I get to work with Brian Allain (Writing For Your Life), Jim Chaffee and Corey Pigg (Chaffee Management), and Paul Tingley (Paraclete Press) on matters of social media and management.

Grateful is dedicated to Roger Freet, once my editor, now my agent, and always my friend.

Finally, the greatest gift I have ever received is that of my family: Richard, who came to me when I least expected such a companion to arrive, bringing with him a lovely son, Jonah, and the surprising gift of our daughter, Emma. For more than twenty years now they have schooled me in gratitude. And they all have plenty to say about every book I write. Without them, and our earthy and loyal dog, Rowan, I would be lost.

Diana Butler Bass
Alexandria, Virginia
Thanksgiving 2017

A THANKSGIVING PRAYER

This prayer was composed in November 2016.

God, there are days we do not feel grateful. When we are anxious or angry. When we are alone. When we do not understand what is happening in the world, or with our neighbors.

We struggle to feel grateful.

But this Thanksgiving, we choose gratitude. We choose to accept life as a gift from you, from the unfolding work of all creation. We choose to be grateful for the earth from which our food comes; for the water that gives life; and for the air we all breathe.

We make the choice to see our ancestors, those who came before us, and their stories, as a continuing gift of wisdom for us today. We choose to see our families and friends with new eyes, appreciating them for who they are, and be thankful for our homes whether humble or grand. We will be grateful for our neighbors, no matter how they voted or how much we feel hurt by them. We choose to see the whole planet as our shared commons, the public stage of the future of humankind and creation.

God, this Thanksgiving, we do not give thanks. We choose it.

And we will make thanks, with strong hands and courageous hearts. When we see your sacred generosity, we become aware that we live in an infinite circle of gratitude. That we all are guests at a hospitable table around which gifts are passed and received. We will not let anything opposed to love take over this table. Instead, we choose to see grace, free and unmerited love, the giftedness of life everywhere, as the tender web of all creation. In this choosing, and in the making, we will pass gratitude onto the world.

Thus, with you, and with all those gathered here, we pledge to make thanks. And we ask you to strengthen us in this resolve. Here, now, and into the future. Around this table. Around the table of our nation. Around the table of the earth.

Amen.

NOTES

PROLOGUE—CONFESSION: NO THANKS

1. Pew Research Center, "2014 Religious Landscape Study," May 30, 2014, http://www.pewforum.org/files/2015/11/201.11.03_RLS_II_questionnaire.pdf.

2. Public Religion Research Institute, "American Values Survey," November 17, 2015, http://publicreligion.org/research/2015/11/survey-anxiety-nostalgia-and-mistrust-findings-from-the-2015-american-values-survey/#.VvVsilJkiLs. See also Jared Yates Sexton's account of the 2016 elections, *The People Are Going to Rise Like the Waters Upon Your Shore: A Story of American Rage* (Berkeley, CA: Counterpoint, 2017).

3. In her book *Radical Gratitude* (Maryknoll, NY: Orbis Books, 2002), Catholic theologian Mary Jo Leddy describes the "culture of craving" as the primary disposition of North American societies today. While I was working on this idea, Rev. Emily Heath, a UCC minister, posted a blog about the "grati-

tude gap" and the 2016 election. Her observations confirmed what I had been seeing as well. See her "Donald Trump and the Gratitude Gap," *Huffington Post*, http://www.huffington post.com/rev-emily-c-heath/donald-trump-and-the-grat _b_11220322.html.

4. Leddy, *Radical Gratitude*, p. 23. It is completely legitimate to be angry if someone takes away something you have or keeps something from you that you need to survive. That is not dissatisfaction. That is injustice, and no one should ever be grateful for that. The full discussion of this appears in later chapters of Leddy's book as well.

5. Dietrich Bonhoeffer, *Letters and Papers from Prison: Dietrich Bonhoeffer Works—Reader's Edition* (Minneapolis: Fortress, 2015), p. 129.

CHAPTER 1—FEELING GRATEFUL

1. Karl Barth, *Church Dogmatics: The Doctrine of Reconciliation* (London: Clark, 2004), pp. 41–42.

2. Philip C. Watkins, *Gratitude and the Good Life: Toward a Psychology of Appreciation* (New York: Springer, 2014), pp. 31–32.

3. The best history of gratitude is Peter J. Leithart, *Gratitude: An Intellectual History* (Waco, TX: Baylor Univ. Press, 2014). Leithart informed my understanding of gratitude and sparked my imagination to think of its future trajectories.

4. Leithart, *Gratitude*, p. 11.

5. Not to mention, of course, the gendered stereotype that runs through such analyses.

6. David Kosten, "The Freedom to Feel Grateful: The View

from Classical Antiquity," in David Carr, ed., *Perspectives on Gratitude: An Interdisciplinary Approach* (London and New York: Routledge, 2016), p. 48.

7. Kosten, "The Freedom to Feel Grateful," p. 49.

8. William McDougall, *Outline of Psychology*, quoted by Robert Emmons in "The Psychology of Gratitude: An Introduction," in R. Emmons and M. McCullough, eds., *The Psychology of Gratitude* (New York: Oxford Univ. Press, 2004), p. 8.

9. Emmons, "The Psychology of Gratitude"; also Robert A. Emmons, *Thanks! How the New Science of Gratitude Can Make You Happier* (Boston: Houghton Mifflin, 2007), pp. 130–31. See also Watkins, *Gratitude and the Good Life*, pp. 78–79. Janice Kaplan, "Gratitude Survey: Conducted for the John Templeton Foundation, June–October 2012." Accessed through "How Grateful Are Americans?" *Greater Good Magazine*, January 10, 2013, www.greatergood.berkeley.edu /article/item/how_grateful_are_americans.

10. Ralph Waldo Emerson, "Gifts," in *Essays: Second Series* (1844), http://www.emersoncentral.com/gifts.htm.

CHAPTER 2—HEART MATTERS

1. Jesse Walker, Amit Kumar, and Thomas Gilovich, "Cultivating Gratitude and Giving Through Experiential Consumption," *Emotion* 16/8 (December 2016): 1126–36; http://psyc net.apa.org/doiLanding?doi=10.1037%2Femo0000242.

2. Walker, Kumar, and Gilovich, "Cultivating Gratitude and Giving."

3. Benedict Carey, "Did Debbie Reynolds Die of a Broken Heart?" *New York Times*, December 16, 2016, https://www.nytimes.com/2016/12/29/health/did-debbie-reynolds-die-of-a-broken-heart.html?_r=0.

4. Robert A. Emmons, *Thanks! How the New Science of Gratitude Can Make You Happier* (Boston: Houghton Mifflin, 2007), p. 66. Gratitude and heart health is Chap. 3, pp. 56–89.

5. Paul J. Mills et al., "The Role of Gratitude in Spiritual Well-being in Asymptomatic Heart Failure Patients," *Spirituality in Clinical Practice* 2/1 (March 2015): 5–17.

6. American Psychological Association, "A Grateful Heart Is a Healthy Heart," April 9, 2015, http://www.apa.org/news/press/releases/2015/04/grateful-heart.aspx.

7. Emmons, *Thanks!* p. 73.

8. Terrance McConnell, "Gratitude's Value," in David Carr, ed., *Perspectives on Gratitude: An Interdisciplinary Approach* (London and New York: Routledge, 2016), pp. 13–14; see also A. Davidson and A. M. Wood, "The State of Psychological Research into Gratitude," in Carr, ed., *Perspectives on Gratitude*, pp. 215–28.

9. Robert Emmons, *The Little Book of Gratitude: Create a Life of Happiness and Wellbeing by Giving Thanks* (London: Gaia, 2016), p. 21.

10. Philip C. Watkins, *Gratitude and the Good Life: Toward a Psychology of Appreciation* (New York: Springer, 2014), pp. 77–78.

11. The Fact-Faith-Feeling Train is so widespread that it is difficult to know exactly where it began or whom to credit. One of its main sources is a tract called "The Four Spiritual Laws," by Bill Bright, of Campus Crusade for Christ. Dozens of variant train images exist online and in print.

12. Robert C. Roberts, "The Blessings of Gratitude: A Conceptual Analysis," in R. Emmons and M. McCullough, eds., *The Psychology of Gratitude* (New York: Oxford Univ. Press, 2004), pp. 58–77.

13. Roberts, "Blessings of Gratitude."

14. Mills et al., "The Role of Gratitude."

15. Mary Jo Leddy, *Radical Gratitude* (Maryknoll, NY: Orbis Books, 2002), p. 61.

16. Henri Nouwen, "The Spiritual Work of Gratitude," Henri Nouwen Society, January 12, 2017, http://henrinouwen .org/meditation/the-spiritual-work-of-gratitude/.

17. Marge Piercy, *Gone to Soldiers*, reprint ed. (New York: Simon & Schuster, 2015), p. 717.

18. "Oprah Talks to Elie Wiesel," http://www.oprah.com /omagazine/Oprah-Interviews-Elie-Wiesel/2.

19. Watkins, *Gratitude*, p. 95.

CHAPTER 3—HABITS OF GRATITUDE

1. Br. David Steindl-Rast, "Practicing Gratitude," www.grateful ness.org/resource/practice-gratitude/. Originally appeared in *Sacred Journey* magazine, October 2001.

2. William James, "The Laws of Habit," *Talks to Teachers* (1899), chap. 8, https://www.uky.edu/~eushe2/Pajares/tt8.html.

3. Charles Duhigg, *The Power of Habit: Why We Do What We Do in Life and Business* (New York: Random House, 2014).

4. James, "Laws of Habit."

5. The Nun Study (University of Kentucky Medical Center) followed a group of Catholic sisters over decades and discovered that those with the most positive emotions (gratitude

included) lived, on average, seven years longer than those who were less positive. Robert Emmons writes about this research in *Thanks! How the New Science of Gratitude Can Make You Happier* (Boston: Houghton Mifflin, 2007), pp. 68–69.

6. S. T. Cheng, P. K. Tsui, and J. H. Lam, "Improving Mental Health in Health Care Practitioners: Randomized Controlled Trial of a Gratitude Intervention," *Journal of Consulting and Clinical Psychology* 83/1 (February 2015): 177–86. See also Emmons, *Thanks!* pp. 27–33.

7. Steve Hartman, "Mother's Job Loss Helps Her Son Recognize His Appreciation," *CBS News,* June 23, 2017, http://www.cbsnews.com/news/mothers-job-loss-helps-her-son-recognize-his-appreciation/. See also Sian-Pierre Regis, *Thank You, Mom!* http://www.goodhousekeeping.com/holidays/mothers-day/a44029/sian-pierre-regis-mothers-day-letter/.

8. There are a number of studies on the subject of mood convergence. See, for example, D. Bernstein, D. Rubin, and I. Siegler, "Two Versions of Life: Emotionally Negative & Positive Life Events," *Emotion,* 2011 October 11:5, pp. 1,190–1,201, www.ncbi.nlm.nih.gov/pmc/articles/PMC3260653/.

9. Robert Emmons, *Thanks!* p. 191.

10. Parker Palmer, *The Courage to Teach: Exploring the Inner Landscape of a Teacher's Life* (San Francisco: Jossey-Bass, 1998), p. 113.

11. David DeSteno, "Gratitude Is About the Future, Not the Past," *Huffington Post,* September 21, 2013, http://www.huffingtonpost.com/david-desteno/gratitude-research_b_3932043.html.

12. Barbara L. Fredrickson, "Gratitude, Like Other Positive Emotions, Broadens and Builds," in R. Emmons and M. Mc-

Cullough, eds., *The Psychology of Gratitude* (New York: Oxford Univ. Press, 2004), pp. 154–55.

13. Fredrickson, "Gratitude, Like Other Positive Emotions."

CHAPTER 4—INTENTIONAL PRACTICE

1. Gregory mentions this practice in a short interview, "David Gregory: 'Opening the Day by Saying Thank You Makes for a Good Start,'" Thrive Global, January 16, 2017, https://jour nal.thriveglobal.com/david-gregory-opening-the-day-by -saying-thank-you-makes-for-a-good-start-e789703902b5.

2. Harriet Kofalk, in E. Roberts and E. Amidon, eds., *Earth Prayers* (San Francisco: HarperOne, 2009), p. 234.

3. Robert Emmons, *Thanks!: How the New Science of Gratitude Can Make You Happier* (New York: Houghton Mifflin Harcourt, 2007), p. 196.

4. E. E. Cummings, "i thank You God for most this amazing," *100 Selected Poems* (New York: Grove, 1994).

5. John Philip Newell, *Praying with the Earth: A Prayerbook for Peace* (Grand Rapids, MI: Eerdmans, 2011), p 12.

6. My family has always been committed to eating the evening meal together. Even with difficult travel schedules and school commitments, dinner was our primary family gathering time. We made it a priority.

7. Sarah Pulliam Bailey, Julie Zauzmer, and Emily Guskin, "When It Comes to Saying Grace, Americans Are Still United," *Washington Post*, June 17, 2017, https://www.washingtonpost .com/local/social-issues/when-it-comes-to-saying-grace -americans-are-still-united/2017/06/16/153e6044–4ade-11e7 –9669–250d0b15f83b_story.html?utm_term=.4e8dd60c860e.

8. Quoted in Robert A. Emmons and Joanna Hill, *Words of Gratitude: For Mind, Body, and Soul* (West Conshohocken, PA: Templeton, 2001), p. 52.

9. Robert Emmons, *The Little Book of Gratitude: Create a Life of Happiness and Wellbeing by Giving Thanks* (London: Gaia, 2016), pp. 22–23; Adam Davidson and Alex Wood, "The State of Psychological Research into Gratitude," in David Carr, ed., *Perspectives on Gratitude* (London and New York: Routledge, 2016), pp. 219–20; and Robert Emmons, *Thanks! How the New Science of Gratitude Can Make You Happier* (New York: Houghton Mifflin, 2007), pp. 33–34.

10. Shai Davidai and Thomas Gilovich, "The Headwinds/Tailwinds Asymmetry: An Availability Bias in Assessments of Barriers and Blessings," *Journal of Personality and Social Psychology* 111/6 (2016): 835–51.

11. Davidai and Gilovich, "Headwinds/Tailwinds Asymmetry."

12. Although it could be another entire book, this discussion could go a long way toward understanding race and privilege. Many white people do not understand the "tailwinds" provided in life by their race and ethnic background. Those tailwinds are largely invisible to them. White people do, as illustrated by my reactions in my story about Elizabeth, however, perceive headwinds and tailwinds based on social class and education. In the United States, people of color have far more headwinds because of race—and precious few tailwinds. The need for laws that provide tailwinds regardless of race (or social class) and systems of justice that do not make for greater headwinds for nonwhite people is absolutely necessary in a diverse, democratic society, especially one with a long history of inequality based on slavery and violence. We

need to equalize headwinds and tailwinds by law for every-one. This needs to be a fundamental task of twenty-first-century politics and communal life.

13. Although many tailwinds are the result of genetic inheri-tance, talent, hard work, or luck, it cannot be stated strongly enough that tailwinds that cause headwinds for others are *never* just. People who benefit from unjust tailwinds need to work to rectify that injustice.

14. Charles Duhigg, *The Power of Habit: Why We Do What We Do in Life and Business* (New York: Random House, 2014), p. 273.

CHAPTER 5—GRATEFUL TOGETHER

1. Robert Emmons, *Thanks! How the New Science of Gratitude Can Make You Happier* (Boston: Houghton Mifflin, 2007), p. 54.

2. Jason Micheli, "Primed for God: Gratitude," Aldersgate United Methodist Church, Alexandria, VA, November 22, 2015, https://www.youtube.com/watch?v=EWkw-dcu2o4. Jason tells his story in *Cancer Is Funny: Keeping Faith in Stage-Serious Chemo* (Minneapolis: Fortress, 2016).

3. Lewis B. Smedes, *A Pretty Good Person: What It Takes to Live with Courage, Gratitude and Integrity* (San Francisco: Harper-SanFrancisco, 1990), p. 12.

4. N. M. Lambert, S. M. Graham, and F. D. Fincham, "A Prototype Analysis of Gratitude: Various Gratitude Experiences," *Personal and Social Psychology Bulletin* 35/9 (September 2009): 1193–1207, http://www.fincham.info/papers/2009pspb-grat-proto.pdf.

5. C. Simao and B. Seibt, "Friendly Touch Increases Gratitude by Inducing Communal Feelings," *Frontiers in Psychology* 6 (June 15, 2015): 815.

6. K. D. M. Snell, "The Rise of Living Alone and Loneliness in History," *Social History* 42/1 (2017): 2–28.

7. See Eric Klinenberg, *Going Solo: The Extraordinary Rise and Surprising Appeal of Living Alone* (New York: Penguin, 2012); Jeanna Bryner, "Close Friends Less Common Today, Study Finds," *Live Science*, November 4, 2011, http://www.livescience.com/16879-close-friends-decrease-today.html.

8. Suggested in Jason Marsh, "What Barbara Ehrenreich Gets Wrong About Gratitude," *Greater Good*, January 5, 2016, http://greatergood.berkeley.edu/article/item/what_barbara_ehrenreich_gets_wrong_about_gratitude. Even Klinenberg, who is optimistic about solo living, admits that certain social and political problems are more difficult to solve in more socially isolated populations.

9. "Gratitude," Google Books Ngram Viewer, https://books.google.com/ngrams/graph?content=gratitude+&year_start=1800&year_end=2000&corpus=15&smoothing=3&share=&direct_url=t1%3B%2Cgratitude%3B%2Cc0.

10. CSPAN, "VP Joe Biden Receives Presidential Medal of Freedom from President Obama," https://www.youtube.com/watch?v=_77ix2o4KbE; see also Greg Jaffe, "Obama Surprises Joe Biden with the Presidential Medal of Freedom," *Washington Post*, January 12, 2017, https://www.washingtonpost.com/politics/obama-surprises-biden-with-medal-of-freedom/2017/01/12/31aa24a0-d90c-11e6-9a36-1d296534b31e_story.html?utm_term=.b5dba370f6b6.

11. Brenna Williams, "Obama Throws Joe Biden the Best Surprise Party Ever," CNN, January 12, 2017, http://www.cnn .com/2017/01/12/politics/joe-biden-obama-surprise-medal -of-freedom/index.html.

12. Shai Held, "The Week That Obama and Biden Cried," CNN, January 13, 2017, http://www.cnn.com/2017/01/13/opin ions/obama-and-biden-cry-held/index.html.

13. Angelina Chapin, "Joe Biden's Tears Show Politics Doesn't Have to Be Macho," *Guardian*, January 13, 2017, https://www .theguardian.com/commentisfree/2017/jan/13/joe-biden-leg acy-tears-politics-masculinity.

14. Smedes, *A Pretty Good Person*, pp. 7–8.

15. Jonathan Haidt, *The Happiness Hypothesis* (New York: Basic Books, 2006), p. 195. Haidt taught at the University of Virginia early in his career. That, no doubt, accounts for the multiple appearances of Thomas Jefferson in his book!

16. Haidt, *Happiness Hypothesis*, pp. 196–97.

17. Haidt, *Happiness Hypothesis*, p. 205.

18. William McNeill, quoted in Haidt, *Happiness Hypothesis*, pp. 237–38.

19. Except, of course, for pacifists—or those who worry about militarism and nationalism more generally. Because of my spiritual and political commitments, I do not often feel very patriotic, but I recognize that others do. Placing patriotism in the frame of gratitude for country seems to steer these sorts of powerful emotions away from the social and political sins of nationalism.

20. "What Is Kama Muta?" http://kamamutalab.org.

Chapter 6—Thankful and Festive

1. Walter Brueggemann, *Deuteronomy*, Abingdon Old Testament Commentaries (Nashville: Abingdon, 2001), pp. 170–78.

2. Brueggemann, *Deuteronomy*, p. 177.

3. Tony Briscoe, John Keilman, and Dan Hinkel, "Cubs Fans Exultant After Nail-Biting End to Championship Drought," *Chicago Tribune*, November 3, 2016, http://www.chicago tribune.com/sports/baseball/cubs/ct-cubs-world-series -fans-game-7-met-20161102-story.html.

4. Nic Flosi, "Cubs World Series Celebration Ranks as the 7th Largest Gathering in Human History," Fox 32 News, November 4, 2016, http://www.fox32chicago.com/news/local /215601786-story.

5. Dave Sheinin, "A Lot of Gratitude," *Washington Post*, April 11, 2017, D1, D5.

6. Barbara Ehrenreich, *Dancing in the Streets* (New York: Metropolitan, 2006), p. 225.

7. Melanie Kirkpatrick, *Thanksgiving: The Holiday at the Heart of the American Experience* (New York: Encounter Books, 2016), pp. 99–102.

8. L. H. Chen and Y. H. Kee, "Gratitude and Adolescent Athletes' Well-Being," *Social Indicators Research* 89/2 (2008): 361, doi:10.1007/s11205–008–9237–4.

9. Nina Lesowitz and Mary Beth Sammons, *The Grateful Life: The Secret to Happiness and the Science of Contentment* (Berkeley, CA: Viva Editions, 2014), p. 6.

10. Lesowitz and Sammons, *The Grateful Life*, pp. 4–9.

11. Joseph L. Price, "In Praise of Play," *On Being*, https://onbe ing.org/programs/joseph-l-price-in-praise-of-play/.

12. Ehrenreich makes this point very forcefully in *Dancing in the Streets*—that big-time sports has been turned into an exercise in consumerist and corporate excess. Yet, she insists, working-class communities in bars and on the streets have kept the practice and experience of sports festivity and play "alive" (p. 245).

13. Seamus Heaney, "A Found Poem," in Cathleen Falsani, "The Unsilenced Voice of Seamus Heaney," *Washington Post*, September 4, 2013, https://www.washingtonpost.com/national/on-faith/the-unsilenced-voice-of-seamus-heaney/2013/09/04/0/ac3c130–1596–11e3–961c-f22d3aaf19ab_story.html?utm_term=.52ff1a10c2c9; originally published in Cathleen Falsani, *The God Factor: Inside the Spiritual Lives of Public People* (New York: Farrar, Straus and Giroux, 2006).

14. Mary Jo Leddy, *Radical Gratitude* (Maryknoll, NY: Orbis Books, 2002), pp. 89–90.

15. See, for example, Jared Yates Sexton, *The People Are Going to Rise Like the Waters Upon Your Shore: A Story of American Rage* (Berkeley, CA: Counterpoint, 2017), on the 2016 election.

16. Ehrenreich, *Dancing in the Streets*, p. 260.

17. Adam Lee, "An Atheist Dinner Benediction," *Patheos*, October 5, 2006, http://www.patheos.com/blogs/daylightatheism/2006/10/an-atheist-dinner-benediction/. Also published in Melanie Kirkpatrick, *Thanksgiving* (New York: Encounter Books, 2016), pp. 230–31.

18. See Alex Vinci, "Thanksgiving Around the World," *Global Citizen*, November 26, 2014, https://www.globalcitizen.org/en/content/thanksgiving-around-the-world/. See also

Kristy Puchko, "How 7 Other Nations Celebrate Thanksgiving," *Mental Floss*, November 16, 2016, http://mental floss.com/article/60261/how-7-other-nations-celebrate-thanksgiving.

Chapter 7—The Grateful Society

1. K. C. Hanson, "How Honorable! How Shameful! A Cultural Analysis of Matthew's Makarisms and Reproaches," http://www.kchanson.com/ARTICLES/mak.html.

2. Jonathan Haidt, *The Happiness Hypothesis* (New York: Basic Books, 2006), p. 47.

3. Peter J. Leithart, *Gratitude: An Intellectual History* (Waco, TX: Baylor Univ. Press, 2014), p. 42.

4. The most thorough discussion of the social structure of gratitude in the ancient world is Frederick W. Danker, *Benefactor: Epigraphic Study of a Graeco-Roman and New Testament Semantic Field* (St. Louis, MO: Clayton House, 1982). Its five hundred–page academic analysis of Greek and Latin terms is not for the faint of heart, however. I also found Samuel L. Adams, *Social and Economic Life in Second Temple Judea* (Louisville, KY: Westminster John Knox, 2014) helpful on social structure, taxation, and gratitude.

5. Leithart, *Gratitude*, p. 49.

6. Danker, *Benefactor*, p. 436.

7. Jane Austen, *Pride and Prejudice*, chap. 56.

8. Colin Wilhelm, "Sanders Taunts Clinton Again on Wall Street Ties," *Politico*, November 17, 2016, http://www.politico.com/story/2016/04/sanders-says-clinton-made-more-in-one-speech-than-he-made-last-year-222058.

9. None of which proved to be true according to the Pulitzer Prize–winning stories regarding these claims by the *Washington Post* journalist David Fahrenthold.

10. Donald J. Trump, Facebook, September 15, 2015.

11. "Annotated Transcript: The Aug. 6 GOP Debate," *Washington Post*, August 6, 2015, https://www.washingtonpost.com/news/post-politics/wp/2015/08/06/annotated-transcript-the-aug-6-gop-debate/?utm_term=.2e45181b2559.

12. Austen, *Pride and Prejudice*, chap. 44.

Chapter 8—Circles of Gratitude

1. Mack Moore, "What Is the Opposite of Quid Pro Quo?" Quora, August 5, 2016, https://www.quora.com/What-is-the-opposite-of-quid-pro-quo.

2. Barbara Ehrenreich takes on this aspect of gratitude in "The Selfish Side of Gratitude," *New York Times*, December 31, 2015, https://www.nytimes.com/2016/01/03/opinion/sunday/the-selfish-side-of-gratitude.html.

3. This point is masterfully made in David Graeber, *Debt: The First 5,000 Years* (Brooklyn, NY: Melville House, 2011).

4. David Steindl-Rast, "What Does It Take to Be Grateful?" TED Radio Hour, *Simply Happy*, www.wbur.org/npr/267202113/what-does-it-take-to-be-grateful.

5. These principles also work in humanism and secularism, in which gifts are seen as the benefice of creation, nature, and creativity instead of God or the gods.

6. Peter Leithart, *Gratitude: An Intellectual History* (Waco, TX: Baylor Univ. Press, 2014), p. 7.

7. Leithart, *Gratitude*, p. 7.

8. Margaret Atwood has a good discussion on the Lord's Prayer and freedom from debt in *Payback: Debt and the Shadow Side of Wealth* (Toronto: Anansi, 2008), pp. 41–80.

EPILOGUE—A CALL TO THE GRATEFUL WAY

1. Quoted in Robert A. Emmons and Joanna Hill, *Words of Gratitude: For Mind, Body, and Soul* (West Conshohocken, PA: Templeton, 2001), p. 52. And yes, I also quote this prayer in chap. 4.

2. Robert Emmons, *The Little Book of Gratitude: Create a Life of Happiness and Wellbeing by Giving Thanks* (London: Gaia, 2016). Another very helpful and practical book by Robert Emmons is *Gratitude Works! A 21-Day Program for Creating Emotional Prosperity* (San Francisco: Jossey-Bass, 2013).

3. Emmons, *Little Book of Gratitude*, p. ix.

4. This list is spelled out with helpful detail in Mary Jo Leddy, *Radical Gratitude* (Maryknoll, NY: Orbis Books, 2002), pp. 142–73.

5. Robert G. Christian III, "The Politics of Gratitude," *Church Life Journal*, September 15, 2016, https://churchlife .nd.edu/2016/09/15/the-politics-of-gratitude/.

6. Albert Schweitzer, *Thoughts for Our Times*, ed. Erica Anderson (Boston: Albert Schweitzer Fellowship, 1975), p. 16.

INDEX